The Grieving Mom

Carol Fisher Akin

"The kinship that comes from knowing someone understands you is the most therapeutic thing the world has to offer."
Jason S. Whitehead

Kindle Direct Publishing
Create Space
Copyright 2021 by Carol A. Akin
All rights reserved. Published2021
Printed in the United States of America
No part of this publication may be reproduced, stored in a retrieval system, or transmitted in any form or by any means—electronic or otherwise—without the express written permission of the author. Failure to comply with these terms may expose you to legal action and damages for copyright infringement.

Library of Congress Cataloging info upon request
ISBN-9798506026617

DEDICATION

This book is dedicated to:

Heather, who made me a mom and a grieving mom

My husband who swam beside me through these deepwaters

My children and grandchildren, who bring me joy

My mom and dad, who guided me

Patsy Farmer, my sister, who was always there to support me

My in-laws, who stood beside us

Paula Barnett, Pam Darnell, and Ann Clay, who flanked my sides to uphold me

Amy Stewart & Venita Cagle who have always held my hand

Wilma Lanier, who took this grieving mom under her wing

Mr. Cochran, who remembered this young couple in our time of need

The very generous Futch Family, whose hearts are attune to the Spirit of God

Our many friends, who have supported and prayed for us

and

Dr. Spark

and all the doctors and nurses at Vanderbilt and St. Jude

who fought for Heather's life

FORWARD

We lost Heather, our 16-month-old, beautiful, precious, baby girl, to a rare form of cancer. How do you wrap your head around that and your heart still beat and your lungs still breathe?

Talk about alone. I was all alone on an island named Despair. There were lots of people waving and shouting at me from shore, but it was all just a blur. I knew they all cared and were trying to reach me. They so wanted to help. But where I now lived was just too far from them. They couldn't possibly understand or reach me.

I longed for someone to talk to—to ask things like: Does it ever get better? Will I ever learn to breathe again—live again? And the big one: God WHY? But there was no one who had answers. I knew my family and friends would empathize with me, but they couldn't possibly understand. Honestly, I didn't want them to hear my pain, see my distress. No one should ever have to share this burden or even witness a wound so deep in my heart. I didn't want my pain to spill out and haunt them. So I put on a smile, and held it all inside.

In desperation, I rummaged through the shelves at the bookstore looking for something to help me, but there was nothing. Years later I worked at Lifeway. I saw a gal quietly slip in and head to the grief section. She thumbed through a few books even as I had done. I recognized the look of pain on her face. Together we searched the shelves and catalog—nothing. It was in that moment God nudged my heart, and I knew I had to write this book. There are moms who are walking this same lonely path, searching for answers to their questions, needing someone who truly understands.

There's a reason the shelves are all but bare on this topic. Professionals try to address it, but we moms are silent. Those of us who have walked this lonely road don't want to open the door and revisit those days, those feelings. We don't talk about this kind of pain. It's a pain so deep you cannot share it. So know this book is written through my tears—for you! I honestly hope my book is never a best seller. I pray no one else ever has to travel this road. But if there's only one, then this book was written just for you. Together we will find safe passage out of the Circle of Grief that entraps us.

THE GRIEVING MOM

TABLE OF CONTENTS

DEDICATION		iii
FORWARD		iv
CHAPTER 1	Life Was Perfect & Then It Wasn't	1
CHAPTER 2	The Jehovah Jireh Takes Charge	8
CHAPTER 3	He Prepares Our Hearts	14
CHAPTER 4	Numbness	27
CHAPTER 5	Busyness	46
CHAPTER 6	I'm Losing My Mind	52
CHAPTER 7	The Blame Game	57
CHAPTER 8	Facing Despair Head On	61
CHAPTER 9	Where's My Spouse?	64
CHAPTER 10	Family & Friends	69
CHAPTER 11	Children	75
CHAPTER 12	Holidays & Anniversaries	78
CHAPTER 13	Mother's Day	89
CHAPTER 14	How To Deal With Their Belongings.	92
CHAPTER 15	The Unexpected & Hard Questions	94
CHAPTER 16	I've Forgotten Who I Am	97
CHAPTER 17	I'll Never Be A Normal Mom	99
CHAPTER 18	An Obsession With The After Life	103
CHAPTER 19	Finding Peace	107

CHAPTER 1
LIFE WAS PERFECT & THEN IT WASN'T
What happened? It's Not Supposed to Be This Way!

Heather was our firstborn, the first grandchild on either side of the family. In fact, we were the first of our friends to have a child. She was much anticipated and dearly cherished. She was the most beautiful, sweet, loving, happy child any couple could ever dream would come into their lives and home. She was simply perfect in every way. I loved everything about being a mother—her mother. It seemed everyone had to stop and notice such a beautiful child and she responded with a smile that would light up any room. Certainly she captured hearts wherever she went. It was so much better than playing dolls as a child. She was vibrant and loving, soft and cuddly, warm and snuggly. She made cooing and gurgling sounds that made me laugh and melted my heart. She was all joy—all mine.

I vividly remember taking her to church for the first time that late July Sunday. Everyone wanted to see her, touch her (yes, we even let people hold our babies in those days). The sun was shining so brightly. As we got back in the car and headed home, I knew this was truly the epitome of the "fullness of joy!" We were young, so in love, and truly blessed! This was just the beginning of a lifetime of joy.

Three months into this amazing new world of motherhood, we had a weekend trip planned with Hank's family to Falls Creek Falls, Tennessee. We were to leave Friday afternoon and return Sunday night. When Heather made her first sounds that Friday morning, I rushed in to say good morning to my little ray of sunshine. Immediately I noticed a bump about the size of a quarter above her left eyebrow. Where did that come from? She didn't have it when we put her to bed. There was nothing in her crib that could have harmed her in any way. As any hovering mom would do, I rushed to the phone to call the doctor. He saidto bring her in as soon as possible. So we dressed and hurried out the door—as quickly as any mom can get a baby bathed, dressed, and in the car with all the things that must go with you on any journey.

Dr. Spark was wonderful. He took us in and examined her carefully. He then uttered the words that would calm the crazy thoughts and fears swirling in my heart and head. "Carol, I think this is a bump that will just go away. Babies sometimes get these little bumps, but they typically just disappear as quickly as they appear. I think you should quit worrying and enjoy your trip this weekend. Keep an eye on it, and let's talk next week if it hasn't just disappeared." I called my husband immediately who was anxiously waiting. I could hear his sigh of relief matched mine.

That afternoon we packed up and headed to Falls Creek Falls and had a wonderful dinner and played board games with our family—all while I kept watching to see if that bump would indeed disappear. The next morning I nursed Heather and handed her over to my mother-in-law who declared she was going to enjoy every minute of her morning with Heather, while we and my husband's siblings and their spouses headed off for a bike ride in the most beautiful color laden mountains any fall had ever painted. And yes, she pledged to watch that bump.

Before we got out of the hotel, one of the gals said she had left her wallet and wanted to go back for it. So we all waited in the passageway (over which the hotel was built) that would lead us out and onto the bike pathways. It was dimly lit, dark even. As I sat waiting on my bike, I turned to talk to my husband behind me. I reached out to steady myself against the wall I was sure was there; but it wasn't. I lost my balance and down I went. I'll spare you the story of my journey through the pain of learning to walk again with a broken pelvis in three places. Suffice it to say, that pain paled in light of the news that lay ahead for us. That didn't keep the tears of intense pain away though. I think these must have been the first of many tears to come.

After spending the afternoon and evening in a local medical facility while professionals did x-rays and an assessment, I was transported back to Nashville to Memorial Hospital on Sunday morning. I hadn't seen my baby since the previous morning. They brought Heather to me about mid-day. That bump was still there. STILL THERE!

I wasn't in the best frame of mind about anything at that point, so we called her pediatrician again—on a Sunday morning—and he took the call. He sounded a lot calmer than I felt. He said, "Carol, Heather is going to be fine. I think you should concentrate on healing for yourself. But I can see you are greatly concerned. Since you are already at a hospital, why don't you have someone take her down for x-rays. Then we'll know it's truly nothing and you can put your mind at ease and concentrate on getting better."

Since my sister-in-law, Paula, worked as a lab tech at the hospital, she volunteered to take her down for the x-rays ordered by the doctor. As she waited outside while the x-rays were completed and read, the doctor approached and asked her if she knew anything about this baby. "Yes," she replied, "Why?" He proceeded to explain to her that there were clearing spaces in the cranial bone. This could be caused by one of two diagnoses, both of which would be fatal for the child. Paula reeled as she struggled to grasp the gravity of this news. What was she going to do? How would she tell us? She took Heather and headed back upstairs. She passed my parents as they were boarding the elevator preparing to return to Huntsville. She panicked. They couldn't leave; I was going to need them. Through tears she poured out the news she had just received. Like her, they were devastated. My dad came to my hospital room door and called Hank out into the hall; and together they shared the news with him. I laid there with Heather in my arms, watching her sleep, wondering what was keeping everyone so long.

After what seemed like forever, but had probably only been about an hour, eventually Hank stepped quietly back into the tiny room just as evening began to fall. When I looked at him I knew something was terribly wrong. The look on his face and in his eyes, not to mention the tears running down his face, sent shivers through me. "Carol, you need to brace yourself. I have some difficult news to share with you." He began to explain all that had transpired: that they had called our doctor and that he wanted to speak with me personally. The phone rang, Dr. Spark said, "Carol, I don't have answers to any of the questions I know you have right now. But I can promise you I'll spend the night researching until I find the answers, and I'll meet you and the family tomorrow morning at ten o'clock."

There are no words I can put on any piece of paper to tell you about the thoughts and horrors of that night and the tears of fear and sorrow. That's not the point anyway. I'm simply trying to share a little of my journey as to how we came to face death, stepping into the Circle of Grief. I call it that because it's like a maze—only once you are in it, you can't find your way out. It wasn't pretty. It wasn't easy. Your journey into the Circle of Grief will be uniquely yours, but no less heartbreaking. It might have been a long journey of illness, a phone call that your child has been injured or killed unexpectedly, or even news that they took their own life. They may be a newborn or 53-years-old. It doesn't matter—you are the mom and you have just lost part of yourself. Just know that I, like you, have grappled with that news and felt that heartbreak.

I am so sorry that destiny now means you are traveling this road. I wish I could show up personally and give you a hug. It wouldn't make everything go away, but at least you'd know someone truly understands your broken heart. Only someone who understands can help bear your burden, and I'd be there to hold your hand and hear your heart as you pour out your sorrow before me. Since I can't be everywhere, know I've written this book so I can put a virtual arm around you to encourage you.

I hope to love on you just a little, as you try to find your footing again. You'll see me struggle and feel my pain. It will feel familiar. Hopefully, in all of this you will find a companion to journey with you as we approach the tough questions.

CHAPTER 2
THE JEHOVAH JIREH TAKES CHARGE

The next few days were a whirlwind of medical procedures. They moved both of us to Vanderbilt where the best medical minds in the country joined in the battle to save Heather. Her diagnosis was Histiocytosis X. I didn't understand what the big word meant, but anything with an X after it was probably not good. We came to understand that she had a rare blood disorder—a type of cancer of the blood. Histiocytes are the vacuum cleaners of the body. They clear away your dead cells as your body is making new ones. Hers were working overtime. They were actually killing her good cells. This would typically be manifested in bone, skin, or eventually vital organs. IF she had been six years of age instead of three months old, her body would be making enough new cells that this wouldn't be a problem. But for a three month old, it was a death sentence.

Our doctor said there were options of places to go, but if she were his child, St. Jude would be the choice. He'd placed the call. They would take her. So, the decision was made to transport both of us to St. Jude in Memphis. I was nursing her and they wanted everything to remain as normal for her as possible. So St. Jude had to admit me when they admitted her. I hold the title for the oldest patient St. Jude has ever had—and my feet hung off the bed because they only had children's hospital beds. It wasn't the most comfortable of arrangements for someone in my condition, but who cared—I could be with my baby. At that point, St. Jude was only a twelve-bed hospital. Their new two-story wing with an ICU unit was under construction. Children were inpatients at St. Jude for a week at intake and then became outpatients staying in local hotels—unless they were dying; then they became an inpatient once again.

Hank sat while I lay on a stretcher in the intake office answering questions. Both of our parents had come with us. They brought the titles to their homes, their checkbooks. Everything we, and they, had was on the line. Nothing was as important as our baby. As the nurse came and took Heather and the aide began to wheel me out, I remembered there was still something important we'd not discussed. "But wait, you didn't tell us what we will owe? We'll give you everything we have." The lady looked at me with the sweetest of smiles and said, "Mrs. Akin, did no one tell you St. Jude's is free?" My head could maleke no sense of that statement. We'd just come from Vanderbilt where I lay on a stretcher for three hours with my baby while my husband had to drive across town to get $3,000 in cash from the banker so they would admit us. FREE—totally FREE? She went on to explain that the local hotels would provide a hotel room for our future visits. There were vouchers for free meals in the cafeteria. Transportation to and from the hospital would be provided if we needed help.

I looked at my husband and our parents. No words were spoken. Tears just ran down everyone's cheeks. It seems there were a lot of tears for a lot of reasons these days. This isn't a commercial for St. Jude, but all I can say is there is no better place here on earth.

The next week was filled with a series of tests, teams of doctors, and ever so many medical terms. It was a crash course in all things Histiocytosis X. There really wasn't much known about this particular cancer. It was so rare only 40 children in all of history had ever been diagnosed with it. Talk about rare. We'd have had better odds of winning the lottery or being struck by lightning. We tried to find the good and embrace as much normalcy and calm as any couple can in a tiny hospital room under these circumstances. We cherished moments. I can still see her laughing as my husband dangled a Fisher-Price apple she would hit with her feet so she could hear the music it played. Oh, yes, she found her feet that week. What fun! We laughed so hard we cried—so many tears yet again! How could it be true she was sick and going to die?

We left a week later, just shy of receiving our doctoral papers in pediatric cancer, with Heather in tow, her first chemo treatment behind us. We'd be back twice a week for the next few months. eventually spacing treatments out to only once a week. And, Dr. Spark was standing by just in case of any emergency.

As we settled into the car, we bowed our heads to thank God for His amazing provision and asked Him to protect us on our journey home. We were just a young couple starting out. We had only been married 18 months. We didn't have big money in any bank account. I didn't even have a job because I'd lost mine during my pregnancy (and no one hired a pregnant gal in those days). Making ends meet was not easy. And now I couldn't walk and my baby was dying. Our families weren't wealthy. Yet we had landed at the one hospital in the world that is free, and it was within driving distance of our home. As we prayed, the tears of gratitude streamed down our faces. Yes, the Jehovah Jireh had provided for us and the baby girl He had given to us; and we were thankful—very, very thankful. So many tears. I didn't know you could cry so many tears for so many different reasons.

Over the next year, there were an untold number of trips back to Memphis. As a young couple, we didn't have the money for gas, but we never missed an appointment. We'd get up, calculating how far we could get with the gas in our tank, trusting God would provide. The phone would ring. Usually it was Mr. Cochran, a widower and retired railroad engineer who lived alone and was a good friend of my dad. He'd ask to speak to me and would ask if we minded stopping by before we headed out that day. He'd slip me $50 before we left and it paid for gas and something to eat on the way. I know heaven welcomed him at his homegoing and there was the biggest of treasures waiting for him because of his many kindnesses and generosity to this young couple.

Before I continue my story, I want to jump ahead just for a moment to Heather's final eleven days while she was in ICU. I got a message that there was a call for me on the payphone at the end of the hall. As I said hello, a familiar voice said, "Carol, this is Oma Mae Futch." The Futch family were dear friends of my parents, and their children had been my playmates—when I was six. I was now twenty-six; it had been a few years. She went on to tell me that when her children arrived for work at their sign shop that morning, she shared I had been on her heart. Her children said they had the same experience over the last 24 hours; I had come to each of their minds. They felt this was no coincidence; after all, it had been 20 years. So they decided to find me. Let's just say there were several phone calls that had to be made to get to that pay phone. She said, "Carol, we know God wants us to send you something. A check for $3,000 will arrive by mail in a couple of days." You could have knocked me over with a feather. That's a lot of money today, but it was a whole lot of money in 1975. It enabled my husband to take off work and be by my side during those final eleven days. Who nudged this family who had not seen me in over 20 years to be so kind and generous toward ME?

Wherever you are in your journey, I hope you look around and see the provision of God for you and your loved ones. I know from experience He's close at hand and actively caring for you. He will send the right people at the right time for you. I even pray this little book will be a source of comfort He can use to bring healing to your heart. Psalms 34:18 tells us "The Lord is close to the brokenhearted." So look around; He's near. He is looking out for you. See if you can spot some of His handiwork.

CHAPTER 3
HE PREPARES OUR HEARTS

I was always struck by the sensitivity of Christ on the cross to those around Him, even those hanging next to Him as they faced death. But most interesting to me was His attention to the well-being of His mother. Obviously, He loved His mom and she loved Him; but, I think it was more than that. There were others present who loved Him as well. He knew, however, there's a special bond between a mother and her children. His mom's heart was compromised in a way only we as mothers can understand. And He comforted her above all others and ensured her care. I feel deep in my soul He has a special place in His heart for mothers grieving the loss of a child.

Heather completed her course of chemotherapy and the clearing spaces went away. By her first birthday she was cancer free and off her chemotherapy. Oh how we celebrated; it was a joyous time. On our next trip to St. Jude for a check-up, however, her cancer had returned and was now in bones in her arm and an organ. It was spreading quickly through her body. They began a new and even more aggressive chemotherapy. We held our breath hoping it would work as well as the first drug.

Heather had been restless all night. She was now 15 months old. When she awakened, I could sense her breathing pattern was just "not normal." Obviously, I called Dr. Spark who had me bring her in at his lunch break. This would ensure she wouldn't be exposed to any illness, and he could concentrate on her. We had a routine down now. He checked her closely and said he didn't hear anything; but thought maybe we should check in with St. Jude. He placed the call and they told us to bring her there. Fortunately, mom joined me and my husband on this trip. When we arrived in Memphis, they checked her thoroughly but didn't hear anything amiss either. They declared, however, they trusted a mother's instincts above their equipment. They wanted to keep her for observation overnight.

The new wing at St. Jude had just been completed. The nurse's station was in the center of the floor surrounded by ten new hospital rooms opening only to the central nurse's station. Each room had a big window on the outside wall that adjoined an ante room for the family. Parents were no longer able to be with their child, but they could see their child and the child could see them. Heather could see and hear us and vice versa. As any baby would do, she sat in her crib, holding her arms up, crying for me to take her; but there was glass between us. So near and yet so far. She pleaded with me to pick her up and I cried silent mom tears. Mom sent me and my husband to the hotel to get some sleep while she stayed in the room adjoining Heather's room. Mom promised to keep a close watch on her and to call me if anything changed.

We climbed in bed, and I tried my best to get some much-needed sleep. But, the best I could do was toss and turn. About 2:00 a.m., I woke my husband and declared I was going to the hospital; I just felt like something was wrong. He reminded me if something was wrong, my mom would have called. I should just go back to bed and try to get some rest. I tried again. By 4:00 a.m, I was frantic. I just knew there was something wrong, and I was going to that hospital one way or the other, whether he took me or not. I'd just catch a cab.

"OK," he said, rather frustratedly. "If you feel that strongly, I'll take you." As we exited the elevator on the 2nd floor of the new wing at St. Jude, my mom was at the payphone. She said, "I was just going to call you. I have no idea what's going on, but for the last few hours there has been a stream of doctors in to see Heather; there's a team of doctors in with her now. I thought maybe you should be here."

Sure enough, thanks to the gentle nudging of the Spirit, I was right where I needed to be. The lead doctor came out and told us Heather had manifested some breathing difficulties during the night. If their assessment was correct, she had a very rare disease called Pneumocystis they had only previously seen with their leukemia patients. Pneumocystis is a parasitical pneumonia. You have 12 antibodies that keep you healthy—things like yeast, bacteria, fungus, parasites, etc.— that must remain in perfect balance (yes, we are fearfully and wonderfully made). Her parasites were way off balance, and multiplying rapidly, clogging the air sacks in her lungs so she could not get enough oxygen. Unfortunately, the news was not good. They had never had a child survive this disease. They were going to x-ray her lungs to confirm their diagnosis and then place her in ICU in an iron lung (the latest technology of 1975). They told us they didn't expect she would live 24 hours if their diagnosis was correct.

My one thought was, "Can I hold her, PLEASE?" No. they didn't want me to pass any germ to her. Now I know the average person would just accept that, but it made no sense to me. IF my child was going to die in the next 24 hours, why on earth would we worry about a germ? Don't you think she'd need her mom?

There was no persuading them. . .or dissuading me. I was going to hold my baby. PERIOD. Since they said they were going to take her to x-ray, I decided it was obvious the x-ray technician (who was no more germ free than I was) was going to take her from the transport buggy and place her on the machine. Then she would have to once again place her back in the buggy. If someone was going to have the privilege of holding my baby for any reason—it was going to be ME! I raced downstairs to the x-ray department and pleaded through my sobs and tears to be the one to pick up and place Heather on that table. Like me, the technician could see there was no logic in why I couldn't be that person. Being a mom, she hid me and my husband in a closet as they brought Heather in. She locked the hallway door to the x-ray room and let us out of the closet. Hank placed her on the table and I got to take her off and put her back in the transport buggy. It was the last time we ever held her. I knew it was our last moment. Oh, yes, there were more tears. Heartbreak unimaginable and indescribable. And immense gratitude to a technician who probably jeopardized her job to allow for this precious moment I've held close to my heart for a lifetime.

It was a Sunday morning and my dad was back in Nashville preparing to preach. He took the call. The congregation understood and insisted he head immediately to Memphis while they held a prayer meeting. Oh how I needed those prayers that day—almost as much as I needed my dad. Several of our church members decided to make the four and a half hour drive each way to Memphis to stand beside us. My sister, Patsy, and best friend, Pam, called their bosses and said they'd be back to work when I came home again. They were going to be with me. PERIOD. There is no greater comfort than my earthly Christian family surrounding us, praying over us. Nine hours of driving just to pray with us. Yes, we were blessed.

Heather was placed in one of St. Jude's two new intensive care units. This was unlike no hospital ICU I've ever seen before or since. One wall was just a big computer screen from ceiling to floor where data was streaming everything about her to the medical professionals who sat at a console in the center of the unit; the two patient rooms were at one end. Behind the console was a glass wall housing a room where the doctors could rest when needed, all while keeping an eye on that wall. If their patient was in the ICU, they were there 24-hours-a-day. Their families were so gracious as their husbands/dads stayed with Heather. They came to visit their loved one and assured us they knew he was right where he needed to be—with Heather. Generous, caring hearts surrounded us on all sides.

So the doctors went into overdrive. We paced, waited and prayed for the longest eleven days and nights of my life. My sister, Patsy, and Pam stayed close to me. We three gals had sung in a trio together since we were teenagers. So we did the only thing we knew to do to pass the time. We sang acapella, three part harmony. Over the next week we went through our entire repertoire of hymns and choruses, which had become fairly extensive over the past decade. Other moms and dads gathered around and sang with us, made requests. Many told us the hymns of their childhood ministered to their hearts as we sang. How do you describe the atmosphere surrounding a group of grieving moms, each watching their child in their final hours of life, singing and praising God acapella, led by three young gals. We exchanged stories, met their children, and entered into their grief as they did ours. So many tears.

There were a couple of children who lay dying whose moms had to be home in Washington state or Michigan caring for their other children. All we could think was those mom's hearts must be grieving in a way even beyond our grief. We were by our child's side, surrounded by our families and best friends, who thankfully stuck close. We were obviously uniquely blessed. There's always someone having a more difficult time than you, if you just look around.

Since we couldn't be with Heather, we three gals took it upon ourselves to become a mother to the children whose moms weren't with them. You'll remember I mentioned children are only inpatient for the first week and finally when they are dying. The second floor was for the children facing death. Death and grief was all around us. Death and grief are always difficult for us humans, but these were precious children. It struck a chord so deep and has left a mark of intense sorrow on my life I cannot erase. Neither can I even begin to describe the life and death moments of that week to anyone. These were intense days of deep sorrow.

The doctors were astounded Heather was still with us. But I wasn't surprised. I knew in my heart it was because I was pleading at the throne of God for Him to save her. People came and went. Calls came from everywhere. And every 20 minutes, 24 hours a day, for the past 10 days, her doctor would step outside the ICU unit, give us a report on her "blood gases" and three times a day he would invite one of us in to see her for ten minutes.

Now I'd love to tell you that in the architect's planning they had created one of those little ante rooms for family members of those in the two Intensive Care Units, but that obviously didn't happen. We sat on the floor in the hallway, backs against the glass outside wall of windows, during those late October days. We hadn't brought clothes to stay. We had no toiletries. We had come to have her checked out and return home. But I sure wasn't going to worry about any of that now. Who needed chairs, beds, blankets, clothes, a coat, makeup or even a toothbrush in these circumstances? I bathed as best one can in a sink in a small bathroom at the end of the hall by the elevators and payphone. No way was I leaving that floor for any reason—not even food. We would just have to make do. I was not leaving Heather.

I think friends must have sensed I needed something more and found a nearby store—who knows? I was beyond caring about mundane things like dress and hygiene. They found snacks and brought in a donut or burger now and then. We survived.

My husband is probably the smartest man I know. He sat there thinking through any possible scenario that might save Heather. Could they do a lung transplant? He'd gladly give her his lungs. No. But I think he surely must have been the first to imagine it, because the doctors scoffed at him; that was not a medical possibility in 1975. Was there something that could dissolve the parasites? Desperation is the mother (or father) of invention. He was full of questions and ideas that I thought were usually pretty ingenious.

While he was inventing new medical procedures, I was focused on praying. For ten days and nights I held a gripping, ongoing conversation with the King of Kings and Lord of Lords. The doctors were in unbelief that she was still with us; I was not. I was in the most intense conversation with God I'd ever had. I'd give Him my life. I'd do x or y—anything He wanted. I didn't care if her brain had been compromised by the huge amounts of oxygen they were administering at that point. Nothing mattered—I wanted my baby girl.

On October 28, 1975, our eleventh day, I got up just before 6:00 a.m. to head to the restroom at the end of the hall. Everyone in our little band was sleeping on the floor. My mother-in-law rose and followed me. I was beyond exhausted. How much more could Heather, or we, take? I closed the bathroom door, got down on my knees by that porcelain altar and begged God one more time for her life. But this time, I said, "Lord, you know what I want. I've made that abundantly clear to you. But, Lord, if it is your will to take her—your PERFECT will, then help me know that it is so. If it is your will, take her now. Right now! And I'll know it is indeed your perfect will for her and me. And I'll accept it. I won't like it. But, I'll accept it." Suddenly a calm came over me and in my spirit I knew there was no doubt about it; Heather had just passed.

I got up, opened the door and asked my mother-in-law what time it was. "Six o'clock," she said. I looked at her and said, "Heather just died." She began to reassure me that had not happened and we should keep praying and believing. "No," I said, "I just gave her to God and He took her." I washed my hands and we walked back down the hallway.

As we were taking our seats back on the floor, her doctor stepped to the door as he'd done hundreds of times over the last eleven days and whispered, "Carol, can I speak with you for a moment?" I looked at him and said, "I think we should wake everyone so you can tell us all together." "Tell you what?" he said, as everyone began to rouse. "That Heather has just passed away," I said with a calm I didn't expect I'd have at this moment. He looked directly at me and said, "How could you know that?" Everyone looked at me in horror, trying to make sense of the scene that had awakened them. "Sir, I'm her mother." He then confirmed that indeed Heather had just passed. Everything had been fine; she'd had a good night. But she just opened her eyes, closed them, and died." I looked at him and said, "And exactly what time was that?" "Six o'clock." He responded. Yes, I gave her to Him, and He took her—immediately took her. His perfect will, not mine.

If you had asked me eleven days earlier, or even the previous evening, if I'd ever be able to stand in any hallway and receive the news of her passing with a calm spirit, I'd have had you declared insane. I should be totally shattered in a zillion pieces. But I was standing, calm, assured of where she was, and confident the perfect will of God was in play. He had wrestled with me for eleven days and nights until I was ready. Can I just say His ways are not my ways? His perspective is not something I can even begin to see.

Looking back, I know He was not surprised by her illness or death. He'd known all about it since before He named her and placed her in my womb. He knew the plan. He knew my heart. And He walked and talked with me those eleven days. He held me. He carried me. He reassured me He had this…and her. This unbelievable calm—was this the work of The Comforter? I now had experienced the peace that passes all understanding. I was standing. Breathing. Talking. As sane as I could be in such a situation. Calm. But strangely enough, there were no tears.

While everyone around me talked, my mind had one question, "Can I trust Him?" I told Him I would. I always thought I could. After all Proverbs 3:5-6 KJV were my life verses, "Trust in the Lord with all your heart, and lean not unto your own understanding. In all your ways acknowledge Him, and He shall direct your path." These words had a completely new and much deeper meaning than I could ever have imagined. Trust with ALL MY HEART! Don't try to figure this all out for myself. Just acknowledge His leading and providing in all my ways and He will direct my path. Well, it was sure a good thing He was going to be directing, because I had no idea where to go from he

CHAPTER 4
NUMBNESS

The first sensation I remember was numbness. No doubt the shock of hearing she had passed, even though we were expecting it as we gathered outside the ICU, left me numb. All I could think of was I now lived in a world my daughter no longer lived in. How could this be? We'd never been separated. This wasn't supposed to happen. Surely this was some sort of horrendous nightmare, and I would awaken soon.

There were people leading me here and there, talking, but I was no longer able to process what was happening or to respond appropriately. Papers appeared in front of me to sign. Questions I never dreamed would be mine to answer were now bombarding me. Did we want to donate her organs? Could they keep her body for 24 hours and run some tests in hopes of helping other children? Who was going to pick up her body and when? Had we made funeral arrangements? I honestly have no recollection of what I signed or said. It was all a blur. My mind was reeling. I sat as still as possible, willing myself not to shatter into a million pieces right in front of them. I desperately tried to focus on their probing questions as if they were the last thread of sanity as my world was crumbling all around me.

Interestingly enough, there still were no tears. Not at this point. Where had all those tears gone? Oh, they'd come later in volumes enough to fill any ocean. But in that moment, I was too numb to feel anything. It was like a giant wall suddenly went up all around me holding back all tears—all feeling.

My husband and I left the hospital hand in hand—without Heather. Where did we go from here? We couldn't even find where we had parked our car or the way to the interstate that would take us from Memphis to our home in Nashville. We no longer knew how to navigate the little things. How were we going to navigate life?

I remember that four hour drive home like it was yesterday. Silence surrounded us like a heavy blanket. There were no words. Nothing to be said. Just silence. And I knew the rest of my life would be like that. Traveling through time as though things were normal, but my heart would be surrounded by a deafening, thundering silence. There was now a vacancy—a vast hole in my heart that had come to abide deep inside me. I knew it would always and forever be with me. And, indeed, nothing has ever filled the void Heather left in my heart that day. My arms physically ached to hold her. There were no words of comfort, no explanations, no answers to our questions. So silence prevailed.

As I looked out the car window, everyone seemed busy, bustling about, chattering, laughing. There appeared to be life all around me, but it was now beyond me. People were living their lives. But my life had been put on pause, if not stopped. Now I could only observe others living. I no longer lived. Oh, my body somehow remembered to breathe, but I now only existed. The world was apparently still spinning for others, but I'd somehow stepped off that spinning world where life, busyness, purpose, and joy seemed to exist for others. And worst of all, I didn't know how to get back on or to even walk away. I became simply an observer trapped in the Circle of Grief.

When we arrived home, Pam and Patsy were there. They had filled the kitchen with food and cleaned the house. I found out later they had even done thoughtful things like my laundry so I wouldn't have to face washing clothing my daughter had worn the day before we went to the hospital. There's no greater gift in life than this kind of friend. They had walked off their jobs and stayed with me while we were in Memphis—for eleven days—as Heather battled for her life. I don't know how to repay that kind of friendship. I've learned I can't. You can only pay that kind of sacrifice and love forward. All I know is if I pick up the phone and one of my friends ever says, "Come!," I'm there.

Pam was in charge now and that was alright with me. People seemed to come out of the woodwork, or maybe it was through the front door. It was hard to tell where they were all coming from. Things were hushed. Everyone hugged me and my husband, uttered something that sounded a lot like they had no idea what to say, and they looked at me with the saddest of eyes. They tried to hide their tears. I had none. I was still in shock.

Everyone wanted me to eat. Where had all this food come from? Thank God there seemed to be enough for everyone. Navigating a restaurant just was not a possibility at this point. Now I knew why people always took food to people who have lost a loved one. I'd always wondered if grief made one extra hungry. I felt like I was moving through space in slow motion. Eating? What was that? Did I know how to do that? Did my throat still work? Food had no place in my life any more. I just couldn't get anything down.

Little by little the house cleared. I remember when Pam left that night, because as she walked out the door to her car, once again The Silence fell around us. Was it always going to be this way?

We lay in bed, listening for any sound that might mean we'd been caught up in a nightmare and our daughter was safe in her crib in the room next to ours. But there was only silence. Deafening silence. Would we ever sleep again? I'm not sure why, but I was afraid to close my eyes. Afraid to cry.

Finally, dawn appeared. Now what? Shortly, my parents arrived. Funeral planning seemed to be the order of the day. We were supposed to get dressed and go to the funeral home to make arrangements. Mom must have found something for me to wear and helped me dress. There was coffee and food, but it still had no relevance. It just couldn't go down. Maybe I had lost my ability to swallow when Heather died. Did death do that to you?

Fortunately, my father was a minister and well versed in funerals and apparently acquainted with the men who ran the funeral home. Decisions had to be made. We had to pick out a casket—FOR MY BABY! Everything within me shouted "NO!" We must have done so because the next thing I knew the funeral director was giving me a time to come back and view my daughter's body and was suggesting I bring burial clothing by at my convenience. Trust me, there is no way to describe the inconvenience of picking out an outfit for my daughter's burial. How do you do that? Where do you go to find that sort of thing? Is there a burial clothing boutique or department that specializes in these things in any store you know?

Mom took charge. It seemed someone had to guide me through every step I took. I didn't seem to know where I was supposed to go or what I was supposed to do next. She took me to a store nearby and the clerk brought out beautiful gowns. Heather had been the first grandchild on both sides of the family so the grandparents and aunts and all my friends had lavished us with everything you can imagine for a child. I'd never even bought her the first outfit and there were dozens of cute things with tags on them still hanging in her closet. But this was my last chance. I was going to pick out the first outfit I ever got to pick out and pay for—and I was going to bury her in it. It just wasn't supposed to be this way. I had dreamed of making the perfect dress for her first day of kindergarten. And oh how I looked forward to going with her and her wedding party to pick out and purchase the perfect wedding gown. But this was never in my dreams and I didn't want it crowding into my reality as it shoved all my dreams aside. All my hopes and dreams seemed to vanish into thin air as I held the sweetest little dress I'd ever seen.

Mom wanted to purchase the dress and shoes, but I felt I had to buy her at least one outfit, even if it was the one I buried her in. Frankly, we didn't have the money, but at this point what was money for anyway? The clerk carefully wrapped it in tissue and placed it in a box. I took the box and clung to it as if it were the only piece of Heather I had left.

Mom drove us back to the funeral home; and I gingerly carried the box in. It was so quiet there. Everyone whispered. Why? Did they hear the deafening silence, too, and were simply hesitant to break it? A gentleman took the box and asked me to wait while they dressed her body; then I could come in and see her. The last time I'd seen her, she was in an iron lung in ICU. Out of nowhere my dad, husband, sister, and in-laws appeared. I guess mom or dad must have communicated with them. All those calls you should make just weren't in my scope of comprehension any more.

As we entered the pink room with beautiful, heavy draperies and thick carpeting, there was the smallest of caskets in the center of the room. Hank took my hand and we approached quietly. The gentleman asked us if we were ready. READY? Can you get ready to view your dead, lifeless child—the happy, bouncing baby you've cherished? Really? You can get ready for that? I held my breath and nodded. There she was—perfect in every way. The most beautiful child in the world. Still. Lifeless. Yet so beautiful in that dress. And the tears began streaming down my face. Tears that had refused to come since I knelt at that porcelain altar and gave her to my Lord, now came like a flood. We stood there frozen. I reached out and touched her hand, the scar above her left eyebrow, her sweet face, her clothing. She was right in front of me, but she was gone.

I have no idea how long we stood there speechless, but at some point someone put their arms around me and led me out of the room.

The funeral director ushered my husband and I into a small room where we sat across from the desk he was sitting behind. Our parents stood somewhere close by. It felt claustrophobic. He said next on the agenda was planning a funeral, a burial…or did we want a memorial service? Who knew the answers to these kinds of questions? It's not like you give birth to a baby and go through funeral planning as if it was the next step after Lamaze classes. We'd just spent eleven unplanned, long days and nights holding our breath as we stood outside an ICU. We were beyond exhausted and not up to any of this. So many questions.

We decided on a private family burial and a memorial service in a few days. Hopefully by then, we could catch our breath and be prepared for such an event. No doubt it was obvious to everyone I wasn't up to anything that resembled a typical funeral and burial service. Our last big event had been our wedding and I'd loved planning every detail. So many hopes and dreams lay before us like a magic carpet ride. But this? How do you plan an event to grieve surrounded by your friends when the light of your home and lives has gone out? There was no more magic in our lives. It was all just too surreal. I felt like we were moving forward, making decisions when there was no more forward, no reason for decisions. It seemed to all be happening around me, to me. However, I no longer could participate or feel anything but an intense sadness that can only be described as complete devastation. Picture a world just bombed until there was only black ash and debris everywhere. It would resemble my new world.

We headed home. Pam and Patsy were there manning the coffee pot and all the food on the counters. So much food—where had it all come from? It felt like God must have multiplied the half loaf of bread and few leftovers we had, turning it into a huge buffet. We sat down in the living room. People came, ate, hugged everyone, cried, and departed.

My dad was a minister. He tried to say the right things to me, but I knew he was as lost in all this as I was. It's one thing to have the right word of encouragement, some spiritual insight, or that perfect comforting verse when you are outside the Circle of Grief, and quite another to try to find any word to utter when you are an insider. You need someone to come along beside you and minister to you, too. You shouldn't be tasked with the responsibility of comforting your daughter when your own grief is almost as great as hers. After all, a grandparent grieves the loss of their grandchild and also has to watch their own child grieve. It's one thing to watch them play ball and lose, but watching them grieve is a whole new ballgame with only losers. There were no prized participation trophies being handed out. Together we simply wept over our loss. As the church organist, I'd played at many funerals of people I'd known. I'd seen death and grief; I'd felt it close in on my heart as I cried tears with them. But I was on the outside looking in. This was different. I'd somehow stepped inside the Circle of Grief.

As we had left the funeral home earlier that day, somewhere deep inside I realized there was the tiniest seed of faith. We didn't weep for her; we knew she was ok. As I looked across the vast expanse of green lawn with thousands of tombstones boasting beautiful flowers in vases, the passage from I Thessalonians 4:13-18 sprang to my mind. I'd memorized them as a child. Oh what a glorious day the resurrection would be.

> *"But I would not have you to be ignorant, brethren,*
> *concerning them which are asleep, that ye sorrow not,*
> *even as others which have no hope.*
> *For if we believe that Jesus died and rose again,*
> *even so them also which sleep in*
> *Jesus will God bring with him.*
> *For this we say unto you by the word of the Lord, that*
> *we which are alive and remain unto the coming of the*
> *Lord shall not prevent them which are asleep.*
> *For the Lord himself shall descend*
> *from heaven with a shout,*
> *with the voice of the archangel,*
> *and with the trump of God:*
> *and the dead in Christ shall rise first:*
> *Then we which are alive and remain shall be caught up*
> *together with them in the clouds,*
> *to meet the Lord in the air:*
> *and so shall we ever be with the Lord.*
> *Wherefore comfort one another with these words."*
> *I Thessalonians 4:13-18*

We had spent over a year worrying about every detail that surrounded her because we knew she was fighting an unseen enemy that was determined to take her life. I had feared every cough, bad day, doctor visits, etc. Was she going to be ok? But I no longer had any concern for her well-being. I wasn't afraid to leave her at the funeral home. If there was a heaven (and I was sure there was one), then there was no doubt she was there—loved and cherished. But we were left behind. As no doubt heaven, and possibly many of the people buried across this acreage, rejoiced right now at her arrival, we mourned a great loss. Two worlds—one rejoicing; the other encased in grief: death. Apparently, we are all dying. Do we just choose to ignore this fact throughout the days of our lives until forced to confront it?

I'd been the mom in charge of her medical appointments and care; I was on top of it all like an obsessed nurse. But now she was ok and I no longer had to spend sleepless nights worrying about her. The problem was that I was not ok. And I was pretty sure things were never going to be ok again. Even simple, normal things (like sleeping and eating), were no longer a possibility.

Some time that afternoon dad said, "I remember the story of how Jesus wept when Lazarus died." He opened his Bible to John 11 and read the story to us. Jesus knew what it was to weep, to mourn. He'd lost His friend. He had been inside the Circle of Grief. While He'd healed many others, this one was personal.

The story reveals Jesus knew Lazarus was ill and at the point of death, yet He delayed His coming. In fact He had quite a discussion with the disciples about His delay. He said one thing that caught my attention, "This sickness is not unto death, but for the glory of God, that the Son of God might be glorified thereby." Apparently Lazarus' death had a purpose—a kingdom purpose? Did Heather's untimely death factor into some plan of God that made absolutely no sense to me but perfect sense from a Kingdom perspective? Let's just say from my vantage point, I could see no purpose worth this kind of loss and pain.

When Jesus arrived in Bethany, about two miles from Jerusalem, Martha came out to meet Him and tell Him that His friend Lazarus had died. Martha went on to say, "Master, IF you'd been here, my brother would not have died!" Yep, she just laid that guilt load squarely on His shoulders. In fact, when she went to tell her sister that the Master was calling for her, Mary arrived with the same attitude and message. You can sense their frustration was at a peak as they had sent for Him and He had not come. Apparently, it's not uncommon to lay this kind of guilt squarely on His shoulders in these circumstances. His message of comfort was one of resurrection and life. He knew exactly what He was going to do to fix this problem. Oh the sisters knew all about His teachings how heaven was the place prepared for those who love Him and how there will be a resurrection and eternal life, but what about their grief now? Even knowing the plan was to resurrect Lazarus, He now joined them in the Circle of Grief, He experienced grief. And He wept.

I so identified with Mary and Martha. I'd prayed so hard over the last year and was a prayer zealot during those final eleven days. Where was God in all of this? Why wasn't He here? Why hadn't He stopped this? He has the power of life and death in His hands. WHY had He allowed this to happen—to me, to us? What had I ever done to Him? I had given my life to the Lord as a young girl, graduated from Bible College, and worked in a Christian school. I'd given God my life. Surely He didn't mean to take MY daughter. WHY was THIS His will? Yep, I understood the sisters. They were hurting—how could He have allowed this to happen to Lazarus—to LAZARUS, His friend who loved Him. To THEM—who had entertained Him, believed in Him, loved Him.

Nothing I knew about love and friendship and God made any more sense to me in those moments than it did to Mary and Martha as they met Him that day. I knew I was standing in the exact spot they had stood, even though I was in Nashville and not Bethany. "Why, Lord? At least help me make some sense of all of this! What were you thinking? Did you not get my message? I prayed and wept before you! Are you sure this was part of your plan? Or, did this one slip up on you while you were busy elsewhere?" At least I knew the answer to this one question because He had taken Heather in a way that assured me His perfect plan was in play.

The most compelling part of this passage is that as they came to the tomb, Jesus wept. Shortest verse in the Bible for a reason. When grief comes and you step inside the Circle of Grief, there are no words. Just tears. This death thing touched Him personally and He wept. Mary and Martha were cloaked in grief. And now that cloak fell around Him. Remember this was pre-Pentecost and the arrival of the Comforter, so they were facing their grief with no Comforter. And Jesus had not been there. So as He joined them in the Circle of Grief and faced the tomb, He wept.

Theologians will tell you all kinds of reasons why Jesus might have wept in those moments. Things like He wept for Lazarus because He was now going to have to leave heaven and return to this fallen world. But in my spirit, I knew He wept because He was in the Circle of Grief where I now found myself. He felt the grief, the expectations of the sisters, and the questions of the crowd. And in that moment He wept. Grief overcomes you. He wept with and for the sisters and loved ones. He felt what it was like to face a personal loss caused by death. It's overpowering. Humbling. It leaves nothing but heartbreak and tears in its wake. He didn't weep for Lazarus; He knew He was about to resurrect him. He wept because He experienced the pain and sting of death: grief.

It may just be me, but knowing this was the last miracle before the cross, I believe it was in those moments, when He wept not only with but for Mary and Martha, that He knew something had to be done about sin's reward: death. Weeping with them wasn't enough. Grief was too painful. He knew the only way to defeat it was for Him to face the cross. He knew the plan—why He had come. He knew what was ahead for Him. But in that moment facing the loss of a loved one, He found the resolve to face and conquer death once and for all for all of us. Yes, He knew my pain. And while He may not show up and resurrect Heather today, I knew why He was able to face the cross. Death had to be defeated. It was too hard to bear. It had to be conquered. It left such great pain and suffering. He had to give His life even if it meant suffering. Oh, He had the power to raise Lazarus this one time, but sin had given death its power and it was ravaging mankind. Only He had the power to conquer it, but it was going to cost Him everything. And He wept. Oh He could refuse to suffer and die, He could save Himself from the cross, He could raise Himself from the dead. He knew all that! But in those moments facing the pain of death, He resolved to move forward, to lay down His life, face the cross and the tomb for us, that we might live again. These days of grief and death would not have the final say. He would nail death to the cross that we might find hope and eternal life together with Him. My favorite hymn had always been Victory in Jesus.

That afternoon I needed a victory and it was only going to be found in Him because of His sacrificial death and resurrection.

{As I type this paragraph, it's Easter morning 2021. I know this isn't a timing coincidence, but indeed a gentle reminder that He's got this life and death thing. Praise God for the resurrection. Easter has become my most precious of holidays.}

Throughout the rest of the day, the words of Jesus to the disciples swirled in my mind, "When Jesus heard that, he said, This sickness is not unto death, but for the glory of God, that the Son of God might be glorified thereby." Heather's sickness had been unto death. But was it somehow meant for His glory? Was God allowing me to suffer even as He allowed the Circle of Grief to surround Mary and Martha for a purpose that would bring Him glory? Was there a plan I couldn't see any more than they could comprehend in those moments? Could I trust Him with Heather? Could I trust Him with my grief? Oh, I had lots of questions. What I didn't have were answers. What I was coming to realize was that faith was something you took step by step; from moment to moment. Yesterday's faith didn't work for today's challenges.

The next day we gathered with our families at the funeral home to bury our baby. My friends, Pam and Ann, joined us. Heather was so beautiful, she took our breath away. There are no words to describe the despair as they closed her casket; I knew I'd never again see her beautiful face this side of glory. Hank and his brothers carried her casket out of the funeral parlor, down the steps and across the way to the burial place. I think normally the funeral home transports the casket with a hearse, but she was so tiny and the casket so small they just picked it up and carried it to the burial site. We gathered in a circle. My dad read a verse and led us in a simple prayer. There were no words to be said, no songs sung, or comfort to be given. And they buried her near the flag poles as we watched. And we departed.

Doctors ordered sleeping pills and we slept. Finally. When I awoke, there was a brief second of awakening when you yawn and are trying to orient yourself to where you are, that I felt calm. Then suddenly, like a roaring, thundering, crashing wave hitting the shore, grief once again crashed into my reality. It was a force so strong I felt it surely must have physically slammed me up against the wall. Would all mornings now be this way? Yes, mornings would be like this for a very long time.

Today was the memorial service. My sister found something for me to wear. Who really cared what. We arrived at the church and had to sit on the front row. A pastor friend of my dad was the officiant. My dad was in the Circle of Grief; he couldn't possibly get through this service. I remember what the minister said as if it were only yesterday, "God was not taken by surprise by Heather's illness or passing. He is still on the throne. He is still in charge. Though your world may be spinning around you right now, He will see you through." This affirmed what I'd felt. God was in charge. He alone is the giver of life and has power to stay Satan's power of death. He is all wise. He is all love. He cares for me. But this is a fallen world.

I didn't understand His ways, but I could trust Him. I would trust Him. Oh, when I get to heaven there's going to be some whys I'll just have to ask. But I'll try to postpone all of those for the present and focus on learning to walk with Him because it had become obvious that without Him, I couldn't take a step forward. I wasn't even sure where forward was any more. That day, sitting on the front row, there were yet more tears. But this time they were different—they were tears of submission to His will. Trusting God isn't for the faint of heart and it's a journey where doubt and fear still nips at your heels. But God had given me Proverbs 3:5-6 for a reason. I would cling to it.

CHAPTER 5
BUSYNESS

Life must go on. Family and friends have to go back to work. The expectation is YOU will go back to work, too. During Heather's days at Vanderbilt, I resided in the orthopedic wing. It was there I met precious Wilma Lanier, a vivacious gal who worked for the VP of a major corporation. She was having surgery on her hand. She noticed the nurses brought a baby in a hospital gown to the girl across the way. She had to find out why. She heard our story and wanted to help. She followed up with me after we returned home from our initial visit to Memphis and offered me a job helping her as a typist. This was back in the day when copies were made with carbon paper. I was an excellent typist. This would allow me to pick up work from her office and bring it home so I could be with Heather. God has angels everywhere and one of them is named Wilma.

My sister bought me an IBM Selectric—the latest and greatest. We had no money, but she was so gracious and generous to me. To put it simply: God provided. This had all worked out beautifully, so I could work at home when Heather was asleep and on days we weren't on the road to Memphis.

But what was I supposed to do now? The last thing I wanted was to stay at home and work. It had barely been a week and I was doing crazy things like suggesting my husband turn down the stereo lest he wake the baby! My mind was playing tricks on me. I'd think I heard her and rush to her room. I knew someday I'd have to address all of her things. But for today, I needed to simply close the door to her room and get out of the house. I needed to go to work somewhere—anywhere—to get my mind on anything but my current reality.

I called to resign from my current position. My friend insisted I now actually come in to the company and continue to work. I tried to dissuade her, reminding her I cried all the time. I wouldn't be much of an employee at this point; and surely it could be difficult to have a crying friend around. She insisted it would work out. They'd just put me in a back room where I could cry all I wanted without disturbing anyone. It was my path forward.

The next few months were spent working. Focusing. I worked hard and long, dreading 5:00 p.m. when I'd have to return home to The Silence once again. Day by day I grew stronger emotionally. Oh, I'd still cry at the drop of a hat, but fewer hats were being dropped. The people around me were busy, they no longer were stopping by to hug me, but rather to pass some piece of paper I needed to address. Complex projects came my way. Travel was required in some instances. Busyness became my way of coping. Oh, I was still trapped in the middle of the Circle of Grief, but I thought my way out was busyness—that 'fake it til you make it' strategy.

At home in the The Silence, I begged God for another baby. Frankly, it felt it would have been easier if He had just left Heather with me. Now surely the least He could do was to give us another child. My arms physically ached to hold her. I needed another child like no mother ever needed or wanted a child. It was an obsession. Everyone I knew was praying for God to give us another child. But month by month, we'd discover that our prayers were not to be answered. And there were more tears.

I was trying to figure this all out on my own. If I could only stay busy enough. If I could just have another child. Surely these things would get me out of the Circle of Grief and I could find life and joy again.

Eventually, we got the news I was pregnant. We were so excited. But then the fear came. What if this child had the same problem? Could lightning strike twice? Could I love this child as much as I'd loved Heather? I knew this child would never replace her, but were we wanting a child to ease our pain or were we really ready to be parents again? Parenting came with a spectrum of responsibility I'd never considered before.

Fear does strange things to you. It keeps you from hoping, dreaming, and planning. It sucks joy from you. The joy of expecting this child was overshadowed by a great fear. I cannot tell you how many times I counted our new baby boy's fingers and toes, examined his belly button, checked him from tip to toe to ensure he was indeed perfect in every way. And, thanks be to God, indeed he was perfect in every way. Fear didn't leave, but I tucked it safely in a closet most days, taking it out only when the lock didn't work so I could obsess over some worry about his health and safety. My children will tell you that even to this day, I'm a gold medalist at worrying over them and my grandchildren. I fear the worst; pray for the best. Other moms never see the danger; they've never experienced how bad the worst can be.

Little boys are different than little girls. He wasn't a replacement for Heather. He was his own very special gift from God. And we cherished him. New babies bring their own version of busy. But busyness of any kind doesn't dispel grief. It fills hours, but it doesn't mend the heart. Joy doesn't dispel grief, and busyness won't cure the grieving heart. Oh, grief can be pushed to the outskirts of your mind, but it's always lingering, and it will invade your heart when you least expect it.

Over time God called me to Himself. He reminded me I needed to be still and know He was God; He was in charge and knows best. I kept so busy; I put off coming to Him. I'd never expected Him to hurt me—to take away my baby. But He didn't condemn me for my thoughts. He quietly kept calling me to Himself. He reminded me there was a balm in Gilead and I was going to find my healing in Him. Oh those were tender meetings with my Lord. But He never failed to reassure me of His love, His plans for me. And day by day, one Scripture at a time, He began mending my broken heart. It would never be the same. He and I both knew that. But those scars were now badges of faith. I came to agree with Job that though He slay even me, yet would I trust Him. I can still hear Rasha Flowers singing Rob Kenoly's "In Everything Give Thanks©: "…but when the tables were all turned around, and Job's world came crashing down, his faith in God caused Job to say, 'I'll still give Him thanks.'" It was through that song I knew I had to come to the place I could thank Him for Heather, even if it meant I would only have her for a few short months, and I'd have to give her back to Him. I like to think He had a precious little one who would only be here on earth for a short while. He looked the world over and chose me for her mother. Thankful for the blessing; thankful for the trial; thankful for the valley. A thankful heart can only come from time spent with Him—not from busyness.

CHAPTER 6
I'M LOSING MY MIND!

Gather the riches of God's promises.
Nobody can take away from you those texts from the Bible which you
have learned by heart.
Corrie Ten Boom

If only I could live in His presence every moment, maybe I could make it. Unfortunately, as I walked around through my days, doubts and fears would creep back in. Sadness and grief seemed to be around every corner. How was I supposed to keep these thoughts, fears and grief from overtaking me? It was obvious I'd never come against an enemy this strong before. Maybe I needed to take a fresh look at the armor of God (see Ephesians 6:10-20). I was struck how verse ten commands us to be strong in the Lord. But my faith was weak, and hope seemed to be beyond my grasp. I felt defeated. I took my dilemma before the Lord and He led me to Colossians 3:

> "Since, then, you have been raised with Christ,
> set your hearts on things above, where Christ is,
> seated at the right hand of God.
> Set your minds on things above, not on earthly things.
> For you died, and your life is now hidden with Christ in
> God.
> When Christ, who is your life, appears,
> then you also will appear with him in glory."
> Colossians 3:1-4 NIV

Now I know the death spoken of here is referencing the death to the power of our sinful nature, but I'm pretty literal and I knew that part of me had died when Heather did. It seemed the remedy for my mental agony was to set my mind on Him and on the Kingdom. Well, that's easier said than done. My mind had a singular focus: my grief. Emotions are hard to wrangle into submission. There was no moment when my mind was at rest. Sleep was all but impossible. I had to find some way to reset my mind because I was sure I was just shy of going completely insane. If Lamaze classes taught me anything, it was that I could endure pain if I focused my mind elsewhere. This wasn't a physical pain, but a mental distress. Maybe it could work for mental torture, too.

I decided to get 3x5 cards and fill them with every verse, hymn, poem, or quotation that spoke encouragement or peace to my heart. I found a large silver metal ring and attached it through a hole I punched in each of my cards. We aren't talking 10-20 cards; that ring housed at least 100 cards at one point, because I just kept adding to it as God gave me another nugget of comfort. Now I could have help available to my ravaged mind at any given time. Those cards went with me everywhere. I slept with them on my nightstand. They sat on the counter as I did my make up or cooked dinner. By day they resided in my purse which I'd take into the bathroom stall and furiously read to get me through the next hour. When driving down the highway, they were right at my side so I could pull off to the side of the road and be reminded of a hymn I could sing at the top of my lungs to drown out all the thoughts my enemy would send my way. It seemed the only peace I could find was quoting a verse, humming or singing a song, reading a poem. I entertained myself for long periods of time as I thanked the Lord for everything I could think of and praised Him for all the good I could possibly name about Him: long lists of things. If the enemy was going to make me despair and struggle with doubt and fear, I was going to praise. I might not be able to conquer death; but, if God's Word says I can conquer my mind by setting my thoughts on things above, then I was determined to do just that.

It's amazing how effective this strategy was. Remember, the Lord said if we resist the devil he will flee from us (see James 4:7). The last thing our enemy wants is for us to trust and praise the Lord, especially in the difficult circumstances of life. So if he's doing anything that causes us to praise, then he's going to quit doing it. Oh, that doesn't mean he won't circle back to see if he can trap you in self-pity and despair again. Just be prepared! I had my cards. I had strength in Him.

I now understood David's heart in Psalm 27:13 when he declared, "I would have fainted, unless I had believed that I would see the goodness of the Lord in the land of the living." Life is hard. Grief is harder than imaginable. I would have given up a million times, but my only path forward was to trust and believe Jeremiah 29:11 was true. He has plans for me. He loves me. He doesn't want to harm me. He is going to prosper us. He is going to take this mess and turn it into something good (see Romans 8:28). Heather had been a gift to me, not a punishment.

I'm 46+ years in. Sometimes I think I see some of what was in His plan. But I'm sure I can't figure it all out on my own, so those whys will just have to wait for heaven. Today, just like every day of busyness for the last 46+ years, I've had to consciously choose rest, which looks a whole lot like trust and faith. I've had to learn to set a guard over my mind and keep it focused on my Lord. This life is but a vapor that appears for a little while and then vanishes away. During this vaporous time we call life, I don't have my baby girl, but I will spend eternity with her. Focus, Carol. Focus on Him and the Kingdom. Some of the verses I memorized are:

Isaiah 41:10: "So do not fear, for I am with you; do not be dismayed, for I am your God. I will strengthen you and help you; I will uphold you with my righteous right hand."

Isaiah 57:15: "For this is what the high and exalted One says—he who lives forever, whose name is holy: "I live in a high and holy place, but also with the one who is contrite and lowly in spirit, to revive the spirit of the lowly and to revive the heart of the contrite."

Jeremiah 29:11: "For I know the plans I have for you," declares the LORD, "plans to prosper you and not to harm you, plans to give you hope and a future."

God will speak directly to you through His Word in ways He knows you can hear. Seek Him. You'll find Him. He's near. There is a Balm in Gliad.

CHAPTER 7
THE BLAME GAME
Casting all your care upon Him; for He careth for you1
1 Peter 5:7 KJV

You may not have noticed until now, but once you become a mom, you are responsible—for everything. That means you get to take credit for any accomplishment of your child. The bad news is you are solely responsible for any wrong decision or any ill that may befall them.

Now it didn't matter that Heather had a rare disease only 40 children in history had ever had. It must be my fault she was now one of those statistics. I had to know the commonality between those 40 children. Apparently, the only thread common to all forty was that the moms suffered some catastrophic event in their fifth month of pregnancy that apparently caused some abnormality of the cell in the fetus. See, I told you; it was my fault.

And because they'd never had a non-leukemia patient come down with Pneumocystis (the second disease) prior to Heather, they realized the disease was not linked to leukemia but to the drug they gave to leukemia patients. So by altering the drug protocol, Heather was the last child to get Pneumocystis. While I was so glad to hear this good news, it didn't help Heather. All I could focus on was that just before I whisked her to the doctor the morning I felt she was not breathing right, I'd given her a dose of that drug. If it was at fault in any way, I had put it into my child, no doubt weakening her body's ability to sustain itself. I was to blame; I'm the mom.

My dear husband was going through much the same grieving process. He was sure he was to blame. While in Vietnam he had been exposed to Agent Orange over and over; maybe that caused an issue with his offspring. He was sure he was to blame for her death and my despair.

Sometimes I blamed others, leading me to hold a root of bitterness. That path I'll keep to myself because I don't want others to carry any blame that is not theirs to bear. Suffice it to say no one was exempt in my determination to find answers. Surely someone or something was to blame.

Oh, yes. You are going to play the blame game. There are no winners in this game. Everyone loses. This is not a road you want to go down. Eventually, it will lead you to blame God, just as Mary and Martha did. Even as I did. You will determine if He had the power, then it's obvious He chose not to use it on your or your child's behalf. WHY?

I remember hearing a horrible story in the news of a mother who placed her child in an oven and killed her baby. I immediately bombarded heaven, "So why didn't you just take her baby instead of Heather. She obviously didn't want her baby! Why me? Why Heather." Yep, God was at fault. He could have stopped all of this. Why didn't He?

Did I mention you'd have questions and they would rear their ugly heads without any provocation or warning? For some reason there just must be someone somewhere to blame. It was as if my mind was not going to rest until I could find a cause and lay this all at their feet. I see parents taking villains to court. Justice is important. Unfortunately, it doesn't bring back their loved one any more than my blame game did for me.

All I can say is, it's a good thing my Lord has strong shoulders. For as He hung there on the cross He took the blame—all of it. He even encourages us in I Peter 5:7 to cast all of our cares upon Him for He cares for us. His shoulders are big enough to carry the blame because His love is greater than all my blaming. He knew we would need someone to blame. How can you stay angry with someone who invites you to blame them?

Over time I came to realize that the giver of life is the Lord. And, while Satan may have power over death, hell and the grave, God has power over Him. He can only go so far (see the story of Job). He numbers our days. He breathed life into Heather's lungs, and He allowed her breathing to stop exactly when I gave her to Him. Yes, He was in charge; the buck stopped with Him. And I needed to trust He had an understanding I did not have and just leave Him with all my cares and anxieties. He knew best. Could I replace blame with trust? It's a step you'll have to make—the sooner the better. The Blame Game is a waste of time and energy.

CHAPTER 8
FACING DESPAIR HEAD ON

So we fix our eyes not on what is seen, but on what is unseen,
since what is seen is temporary, but what is unseen is eternal.
II Corinthians 4:18 NIV

Despair is normal. It's horrible, but it's normal. It's normal to question whether you can go on—will go on. It's normal to come to a breaking point, knowing you cannot take an eternity of mornings with waves of grief crashing in on you. It's normal to want to escape endless long days filled with tears and nights of silence. It's normal to question.

I remember well the pinnacle of those days for me. We were about two months in. I'd tried to keep busy; tried to carry on, but The Silence was deafening. I was alone with my thoughts most of the time with no way to get them out of my head. No one would care if I was no longer around. After all, my arrival to any scene sent people to back rooms to hide their tears. Everyone would be better off without me and I wouldn't have to feel this intense pain any more. I begged God to take me; questioned why he hadn't let me fall and hit my head in some fatal way that day at Falls Creek Falls. Of course I knew the answer to that one; I needed to be with Heather through her tough days. But was I really wanted or needed now?

I stood by my bedroom window, looking up at the sky, pouring my heart out to God. And in my despair the Comforter did more than just comfort me; He reminded me I had many reasons to live. I still had a wonderful husband, a loving family, precious friends. I had future children; who knows, maybe I was even pregnant. It was time for me to count my blessings and find a reason to live again. But it was my choice. Choosing to go on was my choice. It was the right choice. It was the hard choice.

As you ponder your relevance, look around you. There are so many who love you and need you. They are praying for you. It's not going to be easy, but you can press forward. Choose to live. It's the best choice you'll ever make. There's something about grief that holds onto you. It's time to peel away its tentacles that are choking the life and will to live out of you. It's time you choose to live, to find joy in every day be it ever so small: a bird singing, a fragrant flower, a song, a smile from a friend. Look for the joy and make it your own.

Yes, the Circle of Grief is overwhelming. You are going to face despair. But God loves you. He didn't make a mistake. He's still on His throne. You still have a purpose; you just need to start looking outward instead of inward. It won't take you long to find someone dealing with even more difficult circumstances than you are facing. The world isn't easy for anyone. This is a fallen world. God never intended for death to be anything we had to face, but sin changed everything. Now passing through life is going to be hard. But this is not our home; we are indeed pressing on to Higher Ground. But while we are left here, there's good to be done, there are kindnesses to show, there are people who need care and love, and there are people who have lost their way whose hand you can hold.

There's something about helping someone else that is amazingly healing. You just need to face despair head on and tell it to move on down the pike. You've no more time for self- pity. There are too many people out there who need a helping hand. Find a service project, a part-time job, a neighbor with a disability—whatever/whoever. Just do it. You'll find your way out of despair.

CHAPTER 9
WHERE'S MY SPOUSE?

During the eleven days Heather was in ICU, we were visited by a social worker. She took us into a conference room and gave us some statistics on marriage failures for couples who lost a child due to a catastrophic illness. I'm sure the statistics haven't changed much over the years. Bottom line, we were all but doomed to divorce. We might as well bypass all the heartache and just call an attorney when we returned home and file for divorce. It was all but inevitable.

We looked at each other and said, "We won't be one of those statistics! We need each other now more than ever!" Those were words from our hearts—uninformed, inexperienced, naive hearts. Marriages are hard for anyone. There are so many adjustments to be made. Love conquers a lot of things and compromises are key to successful navigation. But we were unaware of the pitfalls that lay ahead for us.

The counselor advised us we were different—after all, opposites attract. Never would we be so aware of our differences than in the way we approached grief. She encouraged us to give each other space and time to grieve in our own unique way because everyone approaches grief differently. We were to learn that truer words were never spoken.

When we returned home, we ran right smack dab into all those differences. I needed to process my thoughts and feelings. I needed to talk about Heather, try to make some sense of it all. I processed my feelings verbally. I cried; and 46 years later, I'm even writing a book—still processing. My husband didn't want to talk about any of it at all. Not a word. He never again mentioned her name, and it's been decades. He put on his headphones and played music as loud as possible to drown out all thought, while I sat in The Silence, forbidden to speak of our daughter. And certainly he didn't want to see me crying.

I looked at him and thought, "You must not have loved her if you can just push all thoughts of her from your mind." And he looked at me and thought, "You must not have loved her if your pain is so shallow you have to talk about it. Mine is so deep I cannot begin to bring it out and address it in any way." The truth was, we were both hurting, but we expressed and processed our hurts in different ways. We were polar opposites. Let's just say there really was no compromise for this; we had no chart to help us navigate these deep waters. My way hurt him; his way hurt me.

The counselor suggested I not talk to my husband about Heather, my grief, or my feelings for at least a year and see where we go from there. Do you remember my mentioning The Silence at home. What were we going to talk about? There was a loss in our home as big as any elephant in any room and we walked around ignoring it as if it had never existed. It drove me insane. I had to get out of the house and talk to someone. Thank God for my mom, dad and friends. They cried tears with me, hugged me, encouraged me. They were my lifeline to sanity.

My husband and I would lay side by side in bed, The Silence surrounding us. All I could think was, "Where was he? Couldn't he see I was hurting? Why couldn't he console me? Why didn't he want to hold me while I cry?"

We'd made vows to each other. My expectation was he was going to be my rock, my fortress in any storm. In reality he could not be there for me because, he couldn't even be there for himself at this time. How could he possibly shoulder my grief when he couldn't even carry the load he was forced to bear? Who was supposed to hold me while I wept if not my husband? Did he not want anyone to hold him? Did he ever cry?

No wonder marriages break down. They are built on unrealistic expectations. Who can prepare you for a valley this deep or a river this wide? All we knew was we were going to hold on. We were going to give each other space and time to grieve in whatever way we needed. We were going to let go of our expectations and dreams in hopes of saving our marriage in the end. We weren't going to judge each other. We knew we had no idea how to make it through this loss; how could we sustain a divorce?

My precious husband was a gift from God. He has been there for me in the good and bad times of life and I'm thankful for him. But even as we are planning to celebrate our 48th anniversary this month, all I can tell you is we are still handling this grief in our own way. We share all the other parts of our lives, but it is rare her name is mentioned—and it is always only by me. Only once did he whisper to me, "Did you remember today is Heather's birthday?" Forty-six years of silence. In all honesty, I'm not even sure I'll ever let him read this book. I may tell him I've written it lest someone mention it and catch him off guard. But you can rest assured he'll never choose to read it. It's not because he isn't supportive. It's just that his way is to compartmentalize things. He has tucked all his grief into a box, locked it tight, and thrown away the key. He cannot allow me or anyone else to open Pandora's box. Maybe you feel the need to get out and socialize, but your spouse refuses to get out of the house. Trust this one thing: you are going to deal with this from polar opposites of any spectrum.

Go easy on your spouse. They aren't perfect. They don't have any more answers than you do. They are hurting profoundly, too. They'll trample all over your feelings and not even know they have done so. But you aren't the only one with feelings. Just tie a knot and hold on. Get help! There's no shame in needing counseling to get you through this. In fact, it's probably the best idea you'll have. You each need a safe place to take out your pain and questions and try to make sense of the chaos in your heart and mind. If your spouse can't go, that's ok. Go for yourself. It's ok to get a tour guide for this uncharted and unexpected journey

CHAPTER 10
FAMILY & FRIENDS

Do not forsake your own friend or your father's friend,
Nor go to your brother's house in the day of your calamity;
Better is a neighbor nearby than a brother far away.
Proverbs 27:10

I have no idea how anyone makes it through grief without friends. They will feed you, eat with you, hold you, listen to all your heart's issues, leave you alone when you need solitude, play with you when you need release, and pray fervently for you. They will be a life line. But trust me, they have no idea what to say to you. They've never walked this path. They have no idea what you are going through. And at some point you are going to realize you don't want them to know. If they could view and feel your grief, it would shake their world and alter them for life. It would change their relationship with their children. Fear would enter their world and never depart. It's not something you can take out and lay on a friend.

Never was this more apparent than on my birthday. Now Heather passed on October 28th. The next week was a blur of all things burial and funeral—not my best week. My birthday is November 8th. I'll never forget walking into my parent's home on the evening of my 26th birthday to the only surprise birthday party I've ever had. There were all my family and friends…with food, balloons, gifts, and gazoos they could blow. This was the biggest celebration they could possibly throw—for me. It was their way of showing me they cared.

But can you just imagine being expected to celebrate anything one week after you buried your child. Really? Maybe in ten years we could find a reason to celebrate something, but in in ten days? I tried so hard not to cry, but it was a losing game. I think most of them thought I was touched by their thoughtfulness, but I was ever more aware of how deep my grief was in the light of celebration. I tried so hard to be what they wanted me to be that night. I blew out candles, ate cake, hugged them all.

But all I could think about was how profoundly unaware they were of grief and its impact on me. I realized during all the coming and goings that everyone wanted to touch me, comfort me, say something to me, but that no one had a clue what to say or do—except Pam who found comfort in manning the coffeepot, food, and the people. But this celebration was cluelessness run amuck.

After everyone left and we returned home to The Silence, I locked myself in the bathroom and wept. There was no one who understood. They all needed to move on. They needed me to move on.

But I knew I'd be forever stuck in the Circle of Grief short of a miracle from heaven, and I wasn't expecting much from heaven at this point. In the stillness, a hymn I'd sung many times came to mind and I began to sing John W. Petersen's "No One Understands Like Jesus©."

." (let's just say being the church organist means you know all the hymns and all the verses to them). I think it's verse three that goes something like "Tenderly He whispers comfort, and the broken heart He heals." I was finding He was a friend beyond compare.

This became the song of my heart. I didn't fault my friends or family because they couldn't fix this. They loved me and were trying to reach me, to comfort me, to help me in any way they could imagine. It was only because they'd never been in the Circle of Grief that they didn't realize their efforts were futile. I'd been outside that circle once with them. They wanted me to come back to them. But they couldn't reach me and I couldn't reach them anymore.

Fortunately, I had some dear friends (Patsy, Pam, Paula and Ann), who didn't try to fix me even though it was obvious I was broken. They were able to balance laughing and crying with me. They didn't call and ask if I wanted to go somewhere (I didn't). They just came by to get me whether I was ready and wanted to go or not. Given my husband didn't talk to me about Heather, they were my sounding board. Oh the mixed up emotions those sweet gals had to listen to and help me sort out. I hope you have a friend in your life. God knew I needed four; one could not have carried my load.

Just let your friends love on you even though they are totally inexperienced in how to do this. I'm not better at finding words to comfort a grieving friend now that I've stepped inside the Circle of Grief than I was before. Like my friends, I just want to shelter my loved ones, drag them away from the grasp of the Circle of Grief. But no one can do that for us. We have to find our own way out. Hopefully you can find a friend with whom you feel safe.

People say bizarre things. My all-time favorite is, "You are still young. You can have other children." WHAT? Do you think I've run out of ketchup and a new bottle is going to fix my problem? Are children just some soiled or torn garment you can toss away and replace with something new from a local store? When people all around you say the darndest things, just smile and hug them. They are doing their best to find something to say that will take your pain away. They are just clueless. Love them anyway.

Jesus is truly the only friend who can walk through this with you. The good news is that He is all you need. His grace is sufficient for every trial, every grief. He whispers peace to your heart at just the right moment and in the right way. My relationship with God became closer than ever during my early days in the Circle of Grief. He was always near; He was always available; He always understood; He always dried my tears and comforted my heart. I learned to talk to Him all day, every day, about everything. He was mine and I was His. He was my rock in the midst of this unrelenting, battering storm. He was all I needed as the winds of doubt blew and the storm of despair raged. He was my hiding place; I was safe in Him. I found I'd run to Him. Day by day I learned to trust Him. My faith was strengthened day by day. Only in the trial is faith strengthened. I didn't enjoy my trial any more than anyone else. But I learned. I grew. And the end result is that I'm more at peace, because I know I have a friend who sticks close to me—a friend on whom I can depend.

There's an iconic picture of The Good Shepherd watching over the flock as He holds one little lamb close to his breast. I am sure I'm that little lamb. I think I love the Shepherd way more deeply than any of His other sheep. While they roam the fields, I just want Him to hold me close, so He does. And, just between you and me, I know He loves me in a very special way, too, because He's held me for so long and so very tightly. He is mine. And I am His. I don't get very far from Him now. He's been my refuge through a mighty storm. He will hold you, too, because I know He is without partiality (see Romans 2:11).

CHAPTER 11
CHILDREN

I'm certainly no expert on how to break the news to siblings or other children in a family or even to friends in your child's classroom. How do you comfort a child's heart through something so great? How do you do that when your own heart is now grieving for them as well as over your own grief? Heather was an only child.

My one piece of advice is you should seek professional help. A professional will listen to your child and help you find a way to help them in the grieving process. It's important you set aside your own personal journey through grief to recognize their grief. I don't think any book can tell you what to do for your child. You are going to need a professional who can pay attention to YOUR child and help you help them with the grieving process. Knowing each of us grieves in our own way, you will have to determine how your child needs to grieve and help them through the process, even if your way is not their way. You'll have to set your way aside to help them. It's called love and it must be greater than your own needs.

I was profoundly struck by how grief affects a child. As we

gathered for Heather's burial, suddenly we realized Hank's youngest brother had disappeared into thin air. He was only ten. Where had he gone? We stopped our plans while several began searching hallways and bathrooms, offices and the outdoors. As the minutes ticked by, panic began to set in. We became more and more alarmed and now everyone, including me, was spreading out in all directions. I lay aside my grief and the gravity of this event to join in the hunt.

I was drawn to the chapel at the far end of the hallway. It felt like it was a block away so no doubt that's why the others had dismissed it. It was unlocked; I opened the door. It was dimly lit with only the light that shone through the stained glass windows. As my eyes adjusted to the dark, suddenly I caught an ever so slight movement. There in the darkness at the far end of the chapel, near a window, stood a little ten-year old boy, weeping. He'd lost his niece and playmate whom he adored. This was his first time in a funeral home. He couldn't bear to see her so still in that casket.

I had no idea what to say or do, so I just walked to him and placed my arms around him, as I knelt down beside him, and together we wept. With a calm I did not own for myself, I assured him though this was hard on us all, everything was going to be fine. We talked about the facts Heather was ok and now with Jesus, and we trusted Him with her. He took my hand as together we joined the others. He ran to his mom and clung to her hand for the rest of the day. To this day I feel ever so close to him—bound together through tears of grief.

So remember to look around you for the children: children of family and friends, playmates of your child, their classmates. Love on these children; they need you and their tender hearts of innocence and pure love will help you heal.

CHAPTER 12
HOLIDAYS & ANNIVERSARIES
"Blessed are those who mourn, for they shall be comforted"
Matthew 5:4 KJV

Let me go ahead and just break the bad news to you. There's no sugar coating it. The first year is going to be unbearable. Holidays are going to be worse than you can imagine. My personal theory is if I plan for it to be bad, maybe it won't be quite as bad as I envision. I had to be prepared lest I shatter into a million pieces.

Since Heather died October 28th, we had put her Christmas toys on lay-a-way in late summer at Service Merchandise and had just completed paying them out in September. Yes, people with no money actually did that back in 1975. We had picked each one out just for her and we could hardly wait for Christmas morning to come. We had safely tucked them away in a closet, where they waited to be wrapped and placed under the tree Christmas morning. We could hardly wait for Santa to come to our house; we were way more excited than Heather would ever be; she was only going to be 18 months old. But, that had not deterred us.

One day about mid-December, it dawned on me: we had all those toys in that closet. They haunted me. They simply could not remain in our home for Christmas. I couldn't bear it. What was I going to do? Obviously, the logical thing was to return them. I'd now wrestled with how to best return them for over a week and Christmas Day was bearing down on us. But who was going to do that? My husband couldn't mention her name. How could I foist the responsibility of returning those toys on him? I'd have to pull up my big girl panties and just do it.

I got a couple of big bags and loaded them up, trying not to look at them lest they bring back the memories of the joy we had dreamed of for Christmas. I loaded them in the car and headed for the store with Amy in tow. Amy was in second grade and I'd adored her and her sister over the years, and they adored Heather. She'd come over to play at my house and I must have thought having this sweet child could help me carry the toys and would distract me, lessening the pain. The store was packed. What did I expect: it was less than a week before Christmas. I kept my head down and headed to the customer service desk only to discover the line was long—very long. Well, so be it. We'd made it this far. We just had to stand in line. No one was looking at us; after all, they couldn't know we were here. They couldn't hear my heart beating so hard and fast—or could they? Just focus. Breathe. I could get through this. "It's just toys!" I told myself.

As the line got shorter and my time was near, I trembled. I kept my head down forbidding the tears to flow. Finally the customer service representative said, "May I help you, Ma'am? You're next." I looked up into the face of a young man in his early 20's. He had a broad smile and was obviously loving his job even in this madness. I foisted my bag of toys up onto the counter and whispered, "I'd like to return these." "Is there anything wrong with them?" he asked. "No. I just need to return them." He took them out of the bag and declared in what seemed like a booming voice, "But ma'am, these are toys; it's Christmas. Why would anyone return toys at Christmas?" He meant nothing by his shocked inquiry, but suddenly there was a silence all around us as everyone waited to hear why the quiet lady with the sad eyes wanted to return all of her toys—at Christmas. As the hush spread through the entire store and all eyes were fixed expectantly awaiting my answer, I said the only thing I could think of—the truth. "My child died." The clerk groaned so loudly. His face reddened and wrenched in pain. He suddenly became quiet, all joviality aside. The crowd gasped and fell even more silent. There I stood in the most unreal of surreal moments, returning my dead child's Christmas presents, clutching Amy's hand, and I didn't know what to do. Tears flowed down my face and I began laughing at the absurdity of the moment—or was I sobbing. I don't know. It was all too bizarre. All I know is I needed to escape. I couldn't breathe. Anxiety was suffocating me.

The clerk handed me my money without another word, and we turned and fled to my car where we sobbed for what seemed like forever. And, yes, of course, suddenly it started raining. Was heaven now crying, too? Why had I done that? Why couldn't I have just let them sit in the closet? Why hadn't I asked a friend to return them for me? Why had I brought a child into this madness? Who knows the answers to all the questions I seemed to find these days. At least by this time I no longer expected answers.

> *"There is a point at which even grief feels absurd.*
> *And at this point, laughter gushes up to retrieve sanity."*
> *Alice Walker*

Holidays are bizarre and the unexpected is sure to happen. At most gatherings you'll be ignored because no one knows what to say to you. They'll speak in hushed tones all around you. It's hard for you and them to merge back into anything that resembles normal.

Showing up at our parents' homes was the hardest time. This was a time when they would normally run out to see us, taking the baby before we could even exit the car. There would be laughter and joy and lots of kisses everywhere. But there was no normal any more. Now they retreated to their room, the bathroom, anywhere to keep from letting us see their tears. It was like I brought this wet blanket to throw on everyone. If only I could find some place to toss it. My parents and in-laws couldn't be there for me any more than my husband. They were trapped in their own Circle of Grief.

Not only are you supposed to be in a celebratory mode for everyone else's sake, but your memories will place your loved one in all things you'd expect for just such a joyous occasion. Never will their vacancy be more profound than at a holiday. Never will you ever feel less like celebrating anything. Family and friends gather and you are most likely needing to find some alone time to process all of this by yourself. But unless you are going to remain locked in the bathroom, there's no place to escape. My favorite strategy was to find something so I could embrace busyness. Could I peel potatoes? Maybe I could wash dishes, clean out the refrigerator, or possibly straighten the silverware drawer—anything to keep busy. It beats sitting on the ottoman watching everyone else talk, work, visit, chase the children, etc.

Whatever your strategy, just know that one year gatherings may bring distraction or comfort; other years you may want to distance yourself from them. It's ok to stay home; it's ok to have an exit strategy and leave early. It's normal for these events to be difficult in times of great grief. There's no need to torture yourself.

Heaven forbid there are other children at any gathering. The little ones will ask about your child because they don't understand why you didn't bring him or her. The older ones will be curious and ask about death. The questions are not so bad from the children. There's an innocence in their demeanor that helps you find words to answer them. And it's in framing those answers in simple ways that you will find some of the answers to your own questions are really simpler than you thought. When you see a child, just be aware that innocence isn't much of a filter for their curiosity.

Be prepared. Church events and family gatherings are always a prime time for a gathering of children. Seeing them can trigger all sorts of emotions. If there's a child that is the age your child was when they passed or would be now, you'll watch their every move. Would Heather now be talking in sentences? Would her hair be that long? Year after year you'll watch and wonder every time you meet a child that is the age your child was or would be. Would she be going to kindergarten this year? Would she have a signature now? Would she be graduating from high school or college? What career path would she have taken? Would she also be a beautiful bride? Would she now be a mother? What talents might she have had? I'll never know the answers to these questions. My only insight is through other people's children. Do they know how blessed they are to spend these days with their child? I do. Heather would be 47 this July 3rd. When someone says they are her age or their child is her age, they always have my undivided attention. I need to soak in everything about where they are at this stage in their life. It's my only way to see her at that age. She might have gray hair now. Hmmm! These are things only a mother ponders in her heart. I remember the Bible saying Mary pondered the things the angel said to her in her heart. Pondering must help mother's make sense of things. Welcome to the world of pondering in your heart. It's stuff we think about and keep to ourselves because no one else on earth would ever believe we can overthink anything this much.

Holidays also bring questions I prefer to reframe as choices. What will you do with her stocking? Will you go to the graveside on her birthday or is it too much for you? Your family traditions will be off in every way imaginable. Your family is broken. This is your new normal and there are no rules. Do you.

I think it helps if you expect things to be abnormal. Maybe you can just throw normal to the wind and take a year off of all things family holiday normal. If Christmas is always at grandmothers' house, maybe this year you go on vacation or eat at someplace you've always wanted to go (if they are open). I found about the only place open on Christmas is a hotel restaurant. I'm good at ignoring holidays if need be. There are no rules—make your own. Do what you need to do to survive. Maybe next year you'll be up to trying to re-establish normal again. This year just focus on the true meaning of the holidays. Try to find things and people for which/whom you are thankful, celebrate the Christ child. Rejoice at the promise of the resurrection.

The difficulty is primarily caused because you've been thrust in the middle of family where tradition and celebration are supposed to rule the day. But families are filled with a spectrum of people from the tender-hearted to the caustic. All of them will be clueless. Just this one year, breathe. It's just a few days. You'll feel as out of place as the store-bought fruitcake amidst all those yummy homemade desserts. But take your place and just breathe.

At some point, you are going to have to settle into "the holidays" without your child. Take time to reflect. Is there a way to honor your child's memory each year—a candle you light? Or is there a special food they loved that you can make and share in their honor? Will their favorite toy now sit under the tree or by the fireplace? Is it a trip to the graveside alone or with family to place flowers? Will you write a poem and read to your family? Do things your way.

This is your holiday, too. There's no guilt—no right or wrong way. Make your own plans. I think recognizing things will be hard and taking control of how you want to celebrate, given the place where you find yourself in the healing process, will help you feel in control when everything seems out of control. And holidays are filled with out-of-control events, conversations, moments, and interactions that you will be totally unprepared to navigate.

Birthdays are by design a time to remember and celebrate. Use them for just that. Remember the good. Celebrate their life and the love you were given. If you view it as a time to celebrate, it will be. Tender, yes; but you were given much. Find a way to honor them.

The anniversary of their passing isn't going to be about just a day. For some reason your mind and body imprints the weather, barometric pressure, and season. Each fall, as the leaves fall, the temperature drops, and the days shorten, I feel a heaviness. I've talked to many others who have lost a loved one, and they experience the same thing. It will sneak up on you. People will say, "You're so unusually quiet." You won't think you are depressed, and hopefully you aren't. You will, however, become contemplative. Maybe we are making room for pondering.

Just remember this valuable piece of advice: It's ok to not be ok. Just hold on. Breathe. Take it one holiday at a time. You'll get through this. The holidays give you time out of the rat race of life to think and process. It's easier to stay busy. Family times are hard to do, but grieving times can be healing as well. Pat yourself on the back as you navigate safely through each one. Hopefully, you'll not have to return toys; you might should find an alternative solution if you find yourself in that situation.

Give yourself some credit. You made it through probably some of the toughest days anyone on earth ever has to pass through. You are stronger than you think. Press on. They'll get easier. They'll never be as you had hoped and dreamed, but they will get easier to navigate. Breathe.

Before we leave this topic, I want us to look at the verse just under the title to this chapter: Mathew 5:4 KJV "Blessed are they who mourn; for they shall be comforted."

There are a lot of things about mourning, but I had never

considered being blessed as one of them. Yet, in mourning, I have felt God's nearness in unexplainable ways and been daily, if not hourly, comforted, which is indeed a blessing. I love the present perfect tense of the verb "shall be." It means we are comforted now in the present and continually into the future. He walks with us, carries us at times, talks to us, comforts our hearts. I've been blessed to have Him so near. Most people are satisfied to know about God and call upon Him in an emergency. I've learned to walk and talk with Him constantly, to lean on Him, to rest in Him. In all this walking and talking, I've gotten to know Him ever more intimately. I am blessed. And He's promised me the best event ever—a reunion. Now that's a holiday that's going to be fun and amazingly awesome.

CHAPTER 13
MOTHER'S DAY

I instinctively knew Christmas was going to be hard. That's why I returned those toys. I tried to have a plan. We made it through-- barely. I prepared for her birthday and the anniversary of her death and we made it through all of them that year. I felt like a runner facing hurdle after hurdle, in a race I didn't want to run and hadn't trained for; so I kept falling flat on my face.

In March I discovered I was pregnant. We waited a few weeks to tell everyone. As circumstance would have it, we announced our good news about the first of May. We were so caught up in the excitement of having a new child, Mother's Day just really wasn't on my horizon. Last year was my first time to be a mother on Mother's Day. She didn't know anything about the significance of that day to me. But I knew my day would come when she was old enough to participate and make me something fun—like pancakes in bed. But those are the kinds of dreams that now I must push aside.

I arrived at church and hurried past the nursery where all the moms were settling their babies. I'd been there with them last year exclaiming over every bonnet and cute outfit, discussing our week with a new child. But no longer was I a part of the group. If I got too close, all conversation ceased as awkwardness settled over everyone. So I hurried up the stairs to the vestibule to find the ushers were handing out red roses to mothers. An usher reached to give me one. Then suddenly, as if he didn't know what to do, he stammered, "Oh, I'm sorry; you're not a mother."

Now this was someone I knew loved me and I loved him. He'd known me since I was a teenager. He'd never hurt me for anything in the whole wide world. He was just caught in that syndrome of not knowing what the right thing was to do or say. I quickly turned aside and found my seat as tears threatened to break loose. I settled in my seat and tried to regain my composure assuring myself I was indeed a mom—a good one. The choir chose to open the service with *"Tell Mother I'll Be There."* Really!? Anxiety began to rise; panic was close at hand. I slipped out of the service, out the back door, and sat on the front steps sobbing. Of course I was a mother. I'd always be Heather's mother. I was a mother who had endured more than any mother should ever have to endure this past year. I deserved some Congressional Medal of Honor for mothering a dying child. I'd earned my stripes—my red rose.

Face it. I was going to end up in tears whether he'd given me a rose or not. It was Mother's Day and I didn't even know if I was still a mother or not. Next year—I'd surely be a for real mom.

Don't let Mother's Day slip up on you. Maybe you could plan a spa day to pamper yourself. You deserve it. Celebrate this day in whatever way is best for you. But remember it's just a day—a day like any other. My husband refers to these kinds of holidays as Hallmark holidays. They were surely made up by this company so they could sell cards.

And take it from me, you are a real mother with or without a rose or pancakes in bed. Well intentioned people are going to say and do all the wrong things. It's not their fault. They've never been where you are. They have no idea they are hurting you. Give them some grace—and reserve some for yourself. As you tuck yourself in bed, praise God you made it through the day with no more than a few sniffles and one breakdown bawling session. And be thankful you don't have a rose sitting around to remind you that you may or may not be a mother.

If there's still tissue in your box at day's end, I'd say you took it like a boss. Keep breathing. Tomorrow will be just a normal Monday.

CHAPTER 14
HOW DO I DEAL WITH THEIR BELONGINGS?

This is really a personal decision. Some may ask a friend to clean out everything before they come home. Others may wait months or years before they open the door to their child's room. Whatever your decision, this is going to be a very emotional activity. There's no practical way you can keep everything. You might make a memory box to hang on the wall. I chose outfits I loved seeing her wear, special toys, etc. and put in a box which I put in the bottom drawer of my nightstand. I've drug that box with me through several moves and across the country. It's my box; my memories.

I found the courage to tackle her things when my sister was expecting a little girl. It was an exciting time for our family and held the promise of new life. Sharing things with her baby just seemed like the right thing for me and her. Probably the most healing thing I did during that time was shop for new baby clothes. I'd avoided the baby department. Now I found it the best place on earth. Let's just say I bought baby clothes instead of spending money on therapy and my niece was well clothed at least until kindergarten..

Looking back, I think setting things right in our home vs having a closed room at the end of the hall, was healing for both me and my husband. Rather than dreading it, I just faced it. I chose a sunny day when I was all alone. I took my time. I held a special outfit close to my chest as if she were wearing it. I could smell the sweet scent of her in the room. It felt familiar and good. It's one of those things that's heart wrenching, necessary, and healing. It gave me a chance to say my goodbyes to her; it gave me permission to move on—at least take a baby step forward.. It's ok to grieve.

Their things are simply memory reminders. Let them bring sweet, treasured memories. But in the end, they are just things your child no longer needs. And since I know your child's memory is imbedded deep in your heart; you don't need these memory reminders either.

CHAPTER 15
THE UNEXPECTED & HARD QUESTIONS

There's just no way you can anticipate and plan for every hard moment. They'll show up unexpectedly. I remember one such moment well. I loved to shop at the nearby mall. Nothing was more fun than to put Heather in her stroller and walk around. I didn't need money—I had everything I needed or wanted in her. Clerks would surround us. Other customers stopped to look at her. If a friend was near they made a beeline to hold her. From day one, all she'd ever known was that everyone wanted to come see her. So if another customer tried to pass by without speaking, she would wave and shout "Hi Dee!" repeatedly, getting louder with each greeting until they stopped and spoke to her. She was the star of my show.

One day several months after her passing, I walked through a favorite store and a familiar clerk smiled and sweetly asked where my beautiful baby girl was today. What was I supposed to tell this sweet, kind, caring person. If I told her she was at home, I'd be lying. If I told her the truth it was going to shatter her as it had the clerk when I returned the toys. But there she was staring at me. I looked away and said, "Unfortunately, she had a rare cancer and is no longer with us." There was the look. The Silence. I thanked her for asking and moved quickly away. Was it always going to be like this? Why did her question pierce my heart? Was it because I wasn't expecting it?

As the years passed and we were blessed with children, someone was always asking, "So how many children do you have?" Now that's a complicated question for me. You see, we lost our first child. Then we had a little boy. While I was pregnant with my second son, we adopted a 6 ½ year old girl. Then two years later we had another boy. And eleven years ago we "adopted" a 35 year old alcoholic whose mom had passed from suicide when he was only twelve. (We'll just leave that story for another time. Suffice it to say, our grieving hearts were bound together as we continued our journey of healing. He's mine now). Try explaining all that. Do I include Heather since she is no longer with us? My children didn't know her. Is it hard for them if I include her. Oh, there are still so many questions with seemingly no answers.

One day someone asked me that question while my four were in tow. To keep things simple, I said, "We have four children." Immediately my oldest son corrected me and said, "What about Heather? There are five of us. Will I count if I die?" Well, that settled it—Heather counted. They all counted. They would always count—even our bonus son. I am the mother to six beautiful children. Question answered from the mouth of a babe. One question down—999 to go.

I don't know how it will best suit you to answer these kinds of questions. Just know they are coming and answer them your way.

CHAPTER 16
I'VE FORGOTTEN WHO I AM
He heals the brokenhearted and binds up their wounds
Psalm 147:3 NIV

In order to survive, your mind has to find a way to move your memory around. I could lose myself just thinking about the pain she endured as I held her through bone marrow transplants and chemotherapy injections. Remembering her in an iron lung or a casket is not how I want to remember her. Fortunately, or unfortunately at times, your brain is going to help you with that.

My oldest son had a car accident when he was 17. He hit a tree head on and we weren't sure he was going to survive. When he came to, he had no memory of the wreck or even that he was driving that day. No recollection of the day at all—not then, not now. Shock has a way of erasing memory.

Losing a child has its own shock factor. In all honesty, I'm pretty sure I also qualify as someone with PTSD (post-traumatic stress disorder). You are going to forget so many of the bad things; cling to special memories. The only problem with this obviously amazing coping mechanism is that you are going to lose a lot of good memories. I remember my parents and sister trying to help me remember a vacation we all took together—the place, the people, the food, the excursions. I got nothing. NOTHING. This happened more often than I'd like to admit. Entire random segments of my past were erased. And, frankly, it will just convince you even further that you are going completely insane. If it doesn't convince you, people around you will begin to question it and may look at you sideways a time or two.

Don't panic. Just gladly relinquish those memories. You don't need them. It will never cease to amaze you how much of your past is gone. GONE! But you aren't going crazy; your mind is just coping. It's completely normal. You've got my word on that. So take a deep breath and feel free to laugh at yourself sometimes.

CHAPTER 17
I'LL NEVER BE A "NORMAL" MOM
*Children are a gift from God; the heritage of the Lord;
hey are a reward from Him"
Psalm 127:3 NLT*

Throughout my years as a mom to our four, there were the typical piles of laundry, carpooling, recitals, games, homework, etc. From the outside looking in, we were a pretty normal family. Everyone in our family was pretty normal—except me. How many times have I heard the words, "Why can't you be like other moms?"

First, you'll find that the typical cuts and scrapes don't tear your soul apart. After all, you've held dying children and held your child through procedures that were painful for her and torture for you. A skinned knee? They'll be ok by the time they marry.

Secondly, serious or even semi-serious medical issues are going to send you to crazy land. If a child has to be hospitalized for some procedure like getting tubes in their ears or some diagnostic test, you're going to lose it. I remember running—RUNNING—out of Baptist Hospital because my son had been taken back for a serious test. I couldn't take any more. I couldn't breathe in that building, so I ran down the hall, the stairs, and out the door. I was in a full-on panic attack. Upon exiting I kept running; I ran all around the huge block on which the hospital resided. I couldn't even force myself to go back in the hospital doors. I stood outside panting, heaving, sure my heart was going to stop at any moment. Then I remembered my son would want to see me when he awakened; so I pulled it together and found my way back to him.

Thirdly, you are going to be obsessively protective. Your children may tolerate your obsessiveness when they are small; but as they get older, they aren't going to know how to handle your fears that something might befall them every time they leave the house. I tried to control my fears as much as humanly possible. They will never know the fear that struck my heart if they were even one minute past curfew. And getting "the phone call" that your child has been in a car accident is the greatest fear for any parent; for me, it was compounded by my previous experience of losing a child because I knew first hand just how devastating that was.

Fourth, you will struggle with letting go. Big Time. When my daughter married we stood by her car after the wedding. I wept, hugged her a half dozen times. Exciting times lay ahead for her; I cried myself to sleep. When my first son got his own place; he was excited; I died a thousand deaths. He felt independent; I felt rejected. When my second son actually left home for college vs. living at home, he went all the way to El Paso, Texas from Richmond, VA. I stood on the back porch engulfed in tears as he kissed me goodbye and turned to drive away. I'd tossed and turned for weeks as I cried in anticipation of this moment. I sat there for at least an hour weeping. I so admire parents who can take their child to college and celebrate with them, holding those tears until they get back in their car. I'm not that mom. He was going so far away. I wouldn't be able to see him. I couldn't open the door to his room, just to hear him breathing as he slept—just to reassure myself he was safe. I was falling apart into a million pieces. Fortunately, my fourth child was only going about an hour away; I held it together a little better. But, since he was the last and now I had an empty nest, there were vast amounts of lonely times to think and grieve in an all too silent house. The days had sometimes been long, but the years were short. There's never enough time to hold your children. Letting go is all but impossible.

Fortunately, I was experienced with grieving loss. I'd start with busy. But could I now trust God with them? After all, He'd taken one of my children; could I trust Him with these precious ones? Let's just say I've bombarded heaven on their behalf every day of their lives and God has had to teach me I can trust Him with them. Letting go is hard if not impossible.

My children are all grown men and women with responsibilities and families of their own. I'm very proud of them all. They all live far away. They are busy with their own lives—as it should be. They'll never know how I yearn to hear their voices, long to hear the details of their lives, and cherish each moment and FaceTime call with them and the littles.

This need to be a mother is deep in my heart, even though my children clearly no longer need a mother. Maybe that's why I've always opened my heart and home to embrace other "kids" who seem to need a mom. I seem to need a child to mother; one to love me even as I love them.

Yep, I'm not a normal mom; and I never will be. Neither will you.

> *"Only people who are capable of loving strongly*
> *can also suffer great sorrow,*
> *but this same necessity of loving*
> *serves to counteract their grief and heals them"*
> Leo Tolstoy

CHAPTER 18
AN OBSESSION WITH THE AFTER LIFE

*And if I go and prepare a place for you, I will come again,
and receive you unto myself; that where I am, there ye may be also.
John 14:3 KJV*

If you are a person of faith, then you have been taught and believe that your child is now in a world you have never seen or visited. Heaven was far away, beyond the clouds. Heaven was not a destination on any itinerary and I had no plans to visit for a very long time. Certainly when that time came, my parents would greet me as my children would continue to live their lives out to a ripe old age. Now my child resided there.

What did I really know about heaven? Let's see: God lives there, angels praise Him as He sits on the throne; the streets are gold, the walls are precious stones, there are clouds, atmosphere, planets, and galaxies between us and heaven. That about summed up my theological perception of heaven.

Now I needed to know everything there was to know about heaven. I researched Scripture, found books to devour, was ever so interested in anyone with a near death or after-life experience. Was heaven real? I had to know she was not in a casket in the ground, but safe in the arms of my Savior. I needed to understand life and death, heaven and our purpose here on earth. I became an avid researcher of all things related to heaven.

Fortunately, the Word says if we seek God with all our hearts we will find Him. No atheist or scientist has any more clue than I did about the afterlife. To embrace their theories one must first believe the Bible is a bunch of made up stories. Their theories were just that; their made up stories based upon their theories. The thing that struck me the most was that they had no hope to offer. Fortunately, I found many scientists who quickly explained all the anomalies of our world that indeed reveal there was a Creator.

I'd studied the Bible in Bible college. One of the first things we studied was the validity of Scripture. I knew all about the founding of our faith and the reasons we know the Bible is the divine Word of God. Why would I spend three years in Bible college studying the Word if I wasn't sure it was God's Word? So we settled that issue in the first two weeks of our studies. I had a starting point. Don't ever let anyone tell you Scripture is not true and then proceed to tell you what they think. Hogwash. Since they have no hope to offer, I'll stick with Moses and the prophets, the disciples' eye witness accounts of Jesus, and the things He told them about the Kingdom of God. Atheists have nothing to offer; my faith gives me hope of an eternity with my baby and my Lord. I can think of nothing worse than getting to heaven and finding one of my children is not there. I'll take my faith any day. Now abides faith, hope and love—I'll take those three any day over doubts and fear of death.

This is not a book about heaven. I'm simply making the point it is normal to want to know everything you can on the topic of heaven. There are some really wonderful books that will confirm your faith and expand your understanding of life after death. Your studies will take away any fears you may have had about death. Faith and hope dispel fear. Did you know that 365 times in the Bible God tells us to 'Fear Not'! I'm thinking He knew I was going to need to hear that every day of the year.

My dad used to tell me the Bible speaks of death as passing through a veil, a curtain so to speak. Walking through a veil never hurt anyone. Psalm 23 assures us that death is just a shadow. Shadows might be ominous, but a shadow never hurt anyone either. And He promises to walk with us and lead us through the valley of the shadow of death.

Life is but a vapor that appears for a little while then vanishes away. Hold on to it; cherish your moments, but know the plan is for us all is to safely pass through that curtain and meet Him and our loved ones.

But as it is written, Eye hath not seen, nor ear heard, neither have entered into the heart of man, the things which God hath prepared for them that love him.
I Corinthians 2:9

Though the mountains be shaken and the hills be removed, yet my unfailing love for you will not be shaken nor my covenant of peace be removed,"
says the Lord, who has compassion on you.
Isaiah 54:10 NIV

CHAPTER 19
FINDING PEACE

God's peace is great enough for our deepest desperation.
You can go on. You can pick up the pieces and start anew.
You can face your fears.
You can find peace in the rubble. There is healing for your soul.
Susanne Dale Ezell

I wish I could tell you that you'll move smoothly from one phaseof grief to the next, putting each phase safely behind you. But it doesn't work like that. This grieving thing is messy. It's uncharted. You'll ask your questions, deal with blame, question God, etc. You'll get some insight or clarity that moves you forward; but before you know it, there'ssomething else that circles back at you. The WHY question is going to dominate your thinking, so let's just go ahead and answer that one. Thereis no answer! And, like it or not, one is not coming. You'll probably never understand it this side of heaven. But that won't keep you from asking the question over and over, searching diligently for some answer to help you make some sense of losing your loved one.

And poor God. He gets a lot of blame. After all, He is omnipotent and He could have prevented all of this, so let's not let Him off the hook too easily.

It had been five plus years. We had four more children. The

house was full and I was busy. But that didn't mean my memories and thoughts weren't ever present with me. I tried to keep them to myself, to cry my tears in private; but the questions haunted me. There was a hole in my heart that could not be filled. And holidays were hard. I was busy now for sure, and that helped mask my grief; inside I was still ravaged. Everyone told me time heals all wounds. Well, time couldn't fix this one. She's not coming back to me whether it's been one year or fifty. I'd conquered looking busy, but the wound was still open and raw; I was bleeding internally. I managed to appear to be ok; I was handling daily responsibilities and busy with a full household. To the casual observer I was on the mend.

That year Christmas was on Sunday. We rose early so the kids had time to open presents and play with them a little, eat breakfast, and get ready for Sunday School. We bought our four-year-old a Fisher Price doll: you know the one where you can button his clothes and tie his shoes. And he loved it; wouldn't put it down. As we prepared to leave, I kept trying various strategies to get it away from him and eventually had to tell him to put it on the bed so it would be there for us when we got home. Nope! He was taking that doll with him. Well, if you've ever confronted a four-year-old, you know there's a tantrum coming straight at you like a freight train at any moment.

Now I knew we had to go to Sunday School, then Children's Church, then across town to Hank's mom's where there would be lots of children and toys, then a stop by his aunt's where her children and grandchildren would be gathered, and finally dinner with my parents where they would be feted with even more toys. There was no way I was going to tack on trying to keep up with that doll. It was best it stay at home until we returned. So, I took the doll, even as he clung to it, and put it in the top of the closet. He stood there screaming, and declared, "I hate you!" Now don't ask me where that came from out of a four year old, because that just wasn't anything I'd ever heard in our home. But I didn't have time to figure that all out—out the door we had to go. And he went kicking and screaming for his doll. Oh, yes, another glorious holiday in full bloom—Christmas Sunday.

The day went as planned. The kids were exhausted by the end of the day and my mom said she'd go home with us and help me tuck the kids in bed, and unload all their new toys; I took her up on the offer. Earlier that evening, I'd told her about my son's tantrum over the doll and asked for her advice on how to handle the out-of-character statement.

As we put the last toy away, tucked each child in bed with a kiss and prayer, and turned out the lights, we took a deep breath. We sat down for a cup of tea and she asked me how I was doing; was this Christmas any easier? I began to pour my heart out to her. "Mom, to be honest, I think things may be worse. I'm struggling. Deep in my heart I know God could have healed her; He knew that was the desire of my heart. I don't know how to say this other than just lay it before you: Right now, I'm ANGRY with God. At times I'm afraid I HATE God. How could He have allowed this to happen to me? I'm a preacher's daughter and a Bible college graduate. I've worked for the church. I'm not supposed to feel this way. So now, on top of everything else, I feel GUILT and SHAME that I am ANGRY with, and may even HATE, God. I don't know what to do!"

In her quiet way, she began asking me questions. "Carol, why did you take the doll away from Jason this morning and put it in the top of the closet? Did you not understand that would distressed him greatly?"

I explained: "Well, I knew how the day was going to go, and I wanted him to have the doll when we returned home. I felt I knew best."

"Do you not think maybe God made a similar decision for you? That maybe He knows what's ahead and He knows best? Let me ask you another question. Why were you not swayed by His distress and give him back the doll?"

"Well, he's just a child. When I told him he could have the doll when we returned home, that seemed like a terribly long time to him, but I knew it was just a few hours so I didn't change my mind no matter how much he cried. It wasn't for forever—just a few hours."

"Carol, do you not realize God's perspective of time relative to yours is probably a lot like your perception of time in relation to Jason's? Could it be God was in a similar position to the one you were in this morning and made the same call? Do you understand He sees your tears and feels your pain, but He still made the hard choice. And let me ask you this. Were you dismayed when Jason said he hated you?"

"No. I knew he just didn't understand. He thought I intentionally harmed him; but I knew I was looking out for him. I love him and understood his heart, so I just picked him up and loved on him until he settled down."

"Baby girl, God loves you, too. He didn't take Heather to hurt or punish you. He took her because, from His perspective, it was the right thing to do. I know it's hard for you to trust Him just as it was hard for Jason to trust you today. I watched you and him celebrate together as you gave him back the doll. And tonight he's fast asleep holding his doll. Do you think you can trust God's perspective? And don't you know He's not angry with you for having doubts and fears, even anger and feeling some hate rise in your heart? He surely looks at you as you did your four-year-old today. There's no doubt He understands you are simply hurting and don't understand what He's doing. You are His child; He loves you so dearly. He just wants to pick you up in His arms and assure you everything is going to be ok, and then go with you as you journey on to life's end where you'll be reunited with her. Maybe it's time you quit kicking and screaming."

Aren't moms great? She knew just the right thing to say to me. That night I gained a new perspective of everything. And sometimes just being able to gain a little insight into the heart and timetable of God can make all the difference. I'm not going to tell you from that moment on I never missed her. I miss her every day. EVERY DAY! And I'm 46 years in now. But what I can tell you is that as I kissed mom goodbye and walked back by the doors of my sleeping children, I thanked God for them and asked Him to watch over them—and to kiss my Heather for me. And I laid to rest all my questions—at least until I get to heaven.

I don't know how God will meet you and answer the questions that tug at your heart, but I know He is anxious to do so. He wants you to trust Him and to be able to move forward in your life in peace. Oh, you'll always remember your child. There will always be one too few stockings on your mantle. But for today—maybe just for today—may you give yourself permission to live in peace and joy, thoroughly enjoying the rich moments and precious gifts that are yours.

>**John 14:27 NKJV:** Peace I leave with you, My peace I give to you; not as the world gives do I give to you. Let not your heart be troubled, neither let it be afraid.

>**Philippians 4:7 KJV:** The peace of God which passeth all understanding, shall keep your hearts and minds through Christ Jesus.

>**Isaiah 17:19 KJV:** "I will give peace, real peace, to those far and near, and I will heal them," says the Lord.

>**Psalm 30:11-12 KJV:** Thou hast turned for me my mourning into dancing: thou hast put off my sackcloth, and girded me with gladness; To the end that my glory may sing praise to thee, and not be silent. O Lord my God, I will give thanks unto thee forever.

*****

Heavenly Father, please comfort the heart of the one holding this book just now in a way only you can do. I didn't market this book or even tell anyone I'd written it. It was simply put on Amazon with a prayer that you would put it in the hands of the one(s) you wanted to heal through the words on these pages. So I'm believing she's been chosen by you because you want her to know you love her and care for her.

It is my firm belief that the kinship that comes from knowing someone understands you is the most therapeutic thing the world has to offer. So I wrote this book to provide kinship, comfort, and hope as you struggle to find footing to exit the swirling abyss of emotions that bombard your heart, mind, and soul. Finding peace looks a whole lot like trusting God. Trusting Him in the face of a devastating loss is the highest most treacherous mountain you'll ever climb; but it's the only way out. Keep climbing.

Lord, now it's up to you to do what only you can do. Hold this special mom close, even as you did me, as you reveal your deep and abiding love for her. May The Comforter come in a new and fresh way and indeed rest upon her. Amen.

O death, where is thy sting? O grave, where is thy victory?
The sting of death is sin; and the strength of sin is the law.
But thanks be to God, which giveth us the victory
through our Lord Jesus Christ.
I Corinthians 15:55-57 KJV

"So it's true, when all is said and done,
grief is the price we pay for love."
E.A. Bucchianeri

ABOUT THE AUTHOR

Carol lives in Lascassas, Tennessee, just south of Nashville, with her husband (Hank) and two pugs (Noah and Sophie). They have six children and six grandchildren. She and her husband love being retired and are active in their church senior ministry. They enjoy cooking, entertaining, day trips, games with friends and neighbors, gardening, and traveling (especially when it means they can see their family). In retirement Carol has pursued jewelry designing, painting and writing.

Connect with Carol at

www.carolfisherakin

or on FaceBook at

https://www.facebook.com/The-Grieving-Mom-102495445365204